Building a
Culture
of
Evidence
in Student Affairs

NASPA
Student Affairs Administrators
in Higher Education

Building a Culture of Evidence in Student Affairs

A GUIDE FOR LEADERS AND PRACTITIONERS

Marguerite McGann Culp *and*
Gwendolyn Jordan Dungy, *Editors*

NASPA
Student Affairs Administrators
in Higher Education

Building a Culture of Evidence in Student Affairs: A Guide for Leaders and Practitioners

Published by
NASPA–Student Affairs Administrators in Higher Education
111 K Street, NE
10th Floor
Washington, DC 20002
www.naspa.org

Funded by a grant from the Lumina Foundation. Developed by NASPA–Student Affairs Administrators in Higher Education. Supported by the West Virginia Higher Education Policy Commission and the West Virginia Community and Technical College System.

Additional copies may be purchased by contacting the NASPA publications department at 301-638-1749 or visiting http://bookstore.naspa.org.

Library of Congress Cataloging-in-Publication Data

Building a culture of evidence in student affairs : a guide for leaders and practitioners / Marguerite McGann Culp and Gwendolyn Jordan Dungy, editors. -- First edition.
    pages cm
 Includes index.
  ISBN 978-0-931654-77-0 -- ISBN 978-0-931654-78-7   1. Student affairs services--United States--Administration.
2. Student affairs services--Research--Methodology--United States. 3. Student affairs administrators--United States. I. Culp, Marguerite McGann.
  LB2342.92.B85 2012
  378.1'60973--dc23
                    2012038687

Printed and bound in the United States of America

Print ISBN: 978-0-931654-77-0

Ebook (ePub) ISBN: 978-0-931654-78-7

Ebook (Mobi) ISBN: 978-0-931654-81-7

FIRST EDITION

CONTENTS

THE AUTHORS

Katie Busby is director of institutional assessment at Tulane University. She is responsible for planning, organizing, and directing campuswide assessment activities as well as coordinating the university's regional accreditation efforts. Before joining the Office of Academic Affairs at Tulane, she was director of student affairs assessment and planning at The University of Alabama, and she held a similar position at Indiana University–Purdue University Indianapolis. She spent 5 years as a member of the mathematics faculty at Baylor University and 4 years as a student affairs practitioner at James Madison University. She holds a BS and MS in mathematics from The University of Mississippi and earned her PhD in assessment and measurement at James Madison University. Busby currently serves as associate editor of *Research and Practice in Assessment* and is an active conference presenter, author, and reviewer.

Marguerite McGann Culp is a higher education consultant; currently, she is partnering with NASPA–Student Affairs Administrators in Higher Education and the state of West Virginia to implement DegreeNow, an innovative project funded by the Lumina Foundation for Education. A former senior student affairs officer and faculty member in Florida, Texas, and Virginia, Culp co-edited *Community College Student Affairs: What Really Matters* (Jossey-Bass, 2005), *Life at the Edge of the Wave: Lessons from the Community College* (NASPA, 1998), and *Promoting Student Success in the Two-Year College* (Josscy-Bass, 1995). Shc has prcscntcd morc than 150 programs at state and national conventions, written numerous book chapters and journal articles, received many state and national awards, and helped more than 50 colleges and universities to build capacity in student affairs, create partnerships between academic and student affairs, and design and implement cultures of evidence.

Brian Dietz is assistant dean of students and director of student involvement at the Hicks Student Center at Kalamazoo College. Previously he was associate director of the L. A. Pittenger Student Center at Ball State University and coordinator of wellness education at Lynchburg College. He has worked in the areas of residence life, late night programming, new student orientation, and student government, and has presented and written extensively on the topic of college student alcohol use. Dietz earned a master's degree in college student personnel from Bowling Green State University.

Gwendolyn Jordan Dungy served as executive director of NASPA from 1995 through 2012. During her tenure, she pursued a number of initiatives to enhance the association's role in building capacity in student affairs, public policy, research, and student learning and assessment. She co-edited *Exceptional Senior Student Affairs Administrators' Leadership: Strategies and Competencies for Success* (NASPA, 2011), co-authored *Assessment Reconsidered: Institutional Effectiveness for Student Success* (NASPA, 2008), and convened the authors for *Learning Reconsidered: A Campus-Wide Focus on the Student Experience* (ACPA & NASPA, 2004). She consults regularly for colleges, universities, corporations, and government agencies on strategic planning and leadership, and presents frequently at national and international conferences.

Beatriz Gonzalez Robinson is vice president for planning and enrollment at St. Thomas University and a professor in the university's Department of Social Sciences and Counseling. In her administrative role, she oversees strategic planning, annual planning and assessment, institutional research, campus emergency management, and student affairs. She is a Fellow of the American Council on Education (ACE), serves on the executive board for the ACE Council of Fellows and on the ACE Women's Network Executive Council, and is a Hispanic Serving Institution Fellow of the U.S. Department of Agriculture. She is the state chair of the Florida Office of Women in Higher Education, a member of the board of directors for the ¡Adelante! U.S. Education Leadership Fund, and an advisory board member for Safe Schools South Florida. She regularly serves as an external evaluator for the Southern Association of Colleges and Schools and was the Latino/a Knowledge Community Chair for NASPA Region III–Florida.

David P. Jones, vice president for student affairs and enrollment management at Minnesota State University Mankato, has also worked and taught at The University of Alabama, The University of North Carolina at Chapel Hill, North Carolina Central University, North Carolina State University, The College of William and Mary, and the University of Nebraska at Kearney. He earned a bachelor's degree from the State University of New York College at Oswego, an MS from the University of Nebraska at Kearney, and a PhD from The College of William and Mary.

Tisa A. Mason, vice president for student affairs at Fort Hays State University, currently serves as director of NASPA's Professional Standards Division. Mason earned a doctorate in education from The College of William and Mary; she received the Galfo Research Award, which is given annually to the graduate student who has demonstrated outstanding promise in educational research and helpfulness to fellow students. Her master's degree is from Eastern Illinois University and her bachelor's from Transylvania University.

Shana Warkentine Meyer is assistant vice president for student affairs at Fort Hays State University, where she oversees the leadership of the Student Life Cluster, an area that includes Diversity Affairs, the Memorial Union, the Center for Student Involvement and Student Organizations, Special Events, Greek Life, Residential Life, the Student Governing Association, International Student Services, Disability Student Services, Tiger Tots Nurtury Center, Judicial Affairs, and First Year Experience.

She earned a BS in English/journalism and an MS in counselor education with an emphasis on student personnel from Emporia State University and has completed the coursework at Kansas State University toward a PhD in student affairs in higher education.

Kathryn Mueller is dean of student services at Orange Coast College in Costa Mesa, California, and director of NASPA's Community Colleges Division. Mueller has more than 26 years of experience in student affairs and higher education in large, small, private, and public institutions, as well as four-year and community colleges. She has a doctorate in educational leadership and higher education from the University of Nebraska–Lincoln. She is the lead for student learning outcomes and program review at Orange Coast College and has provided numerous workshops, trainings, and consultations for colleagues and institutions on these subjects.

Lori E. Varlotta is executive vice president for planning, enrollment management, and student affairs at California State University, Sacramento, where she leads a student affairs division that has created and implemented a nationally recognized outcomes-based assessment program, an acclaimed student veterans program, a comprehensive student athlete resource center, and The WELL—an integrated collegiate recreation and wellness facility. Beyond the campus, Varlotta contributes to the state and national conversation on higher education assessment, accountability, budgeting, and student health by frequently publishing and presenting on these topics. A first-generation college student, she earned a BA in philosophy from the University of Notre Dame, an MA from Syracuse University, and an interdisciplinary PhD from Miami University.

Andrew F. Wall is associate professor of higher education and chair of the Department of Educational Leadership in the University of Rochester's Warner School of Education and Human Development where he teaches courses in organization and governance of higher education, higher education policy, and evaluation in higher education. He is a Young Academic Fellow for the Institute for Higher Education Policy and the Lumina Foundation for Education. Wall focuses his research and evaluation projects in the areas of college student health and learning, learning outcomes, state educational finance, and public trust in education. His research has appeared in the *Journal of College Student Development, Journal of Education Finance, Policy Futures in Education, Community College Review, Journal of Student Affairs Research and Practice, Journal of Psychology: Interdisciplinary and Applied,* and *Journal of Diversity in Higher Education.* Wall co-authored *Assessment Reconsidered: Institutional Effectiveness for Student Success* (NASPA, 2008) and was named an Emerging Scholar by the American College Personnel Association in 2008.

MODULE 1

Starting the Culture of Evidence Journey

Marguerite McGann Culp

BUILDING CULTURES OF EVIDENCE in student affairs is nothing new. Since 1937, student affairs professionals have used a variety of strategies to demonstrate how their programs, processes, and services contribute to higher education's bottom line: student access and student success. What *is* new is the increasing complexity of student affairs responsibilities, escalating expectations for the profession, and an unprecedented proliferation of tools to measure the effectiveness of processes, programs, and services. To respond to these challenges, student affairs professionals are seeking assistance in a variety of areas, from identifying gaps in their knowledge base and skill sets to conceptualizing what a well-developed culture of evidence looks like. This first module of *Building a Culture of Evidence in Student Affairs: A Guide for Leaders and Practitioners* offers a starting point by providing self-assessment instruments, a culture of evidence road map, and words of wisdom from presidents and senior student affairs officers (SSAOs). It also features snapshots of the other modules in the guide.

Cultures of evidence offer student affairs professionals opportunities to examine their work; make it more effective and efficient; and increase the probability that they will design and implement programs, processes, and services that really matter. Operating within a culture of evidence also allows student affairs professionals to remain in a continuous professional and personal learning loop: asking questions that matter; building on successes; learning from failures; and designing and implementing programs, processes, and services to help students define and reach their educational and career goals. Cultures of evidence also offer a degree of protection for student affairs professionals, as they document with hard data the significant contributions student affairs makes toward the institution's mission and goals.

EVOLUTION OF THE CULTURE OF EVIDENCE

Some student affairs professionals reminisce about working in colleges and universities BCE (before the culture of evidence era). Others talk about a "culture of evidence revolution." Neither perspective is completely accurate. The student affairs profession is in the midst of a culture of evidence *evolution*, not revolution; the emphasis on assessment and outcomes has been around since the dawn of the profession. In June 1937, *The Student Personnel Point of View* outlined expectations and values for the fledgling profession. Of the 23 expectations, 5 stressed the need to evaluate and conduct studies to improve student personnel functions and services. The revised *Student Personnel Point of View*, published in 1949, called for "a continuing program of evaluation of student personnel services . . . to ensure the achievement by students of the objectives for which the program is designed" (p. 8) and suggested criteria that practitioners could use to assess the effectiveness of programs and services. In the 1960s, 10 student affairs associations created the Council of Student Personnel Associations in Higher Education (COSPA) to establish standards to guide practice and preparation. Although COSPA was dissolved in 1976, it paved the way for the establishment in 1979 of the Council for the Advancement of Standards for Student Services/Development Programs. Now known as the Council for the Advancement of Standards in Higher Education (CAS), it includes more than 40 professional associations. Among its many contributions to the profession, CAS created and is responsible for periodically updating the *CAS Standards* (2012), a document that outlines detailed expectations and outcomes for major functional areas in student affairs; the *CAS Self-Assessment Guides* (2012), functional area self-assessment guides coupled with a PowerPoint presentation and an e-learning course for conducting assessments; and the *Frameworks for Assessing Learning and Developmental Outcomes* (2006), a description of learning outcomes, assessment examples, and assessment tools. Although currently out of print, the *Frameworks for Assessing Learning and Developmental Outcomes* (2006) is available as a downloadable PDF.

QUICK TIP

"It is important to be clear about the aims of a culture of evidence. The goal is to use evidence to better understand our students and their experiences so we can improve our work with them." —*Sarah Westfall, vice president for student development and dean of students, Kalamazoo College (personal communication, May 24, 2012)*

RISK-REWARD CONTINUUM

Results of surveys conducted by NASPA–Student Affairs Administrators in Higher Education and feedback from participants in the Culture of Evidence/Student Learning Outcomes workshop offered before the NASPA Assessment and Persistence Conferences in 2010, 2011, and 2012 indicate that many professionals understand the importance of establishing a culture of evidence in student affairs but struggle with the logistics of designing and implementing such a culture at their institutions. The role of outcomes (developmental, learning, and program) seems especially challenging; the selection of appropriate assessment tools is perceived as a demanding task; and building capacity in student affairs is viewed as a time-consuming and expensive endeavor. Table 1.1 shows how student affairs professionals view the risks and rewards associated with building cultures of evidence. In the final analysis, however, student affairs leaders view the creation of data-based and outcomes-oriented programs and services as a critical need, a major professional responsibility, and, most important, the right thing to do (Culp 2012).

Table 1.1

Risks and Rewards Associated With Creating a Culture of Evidence in Student Affairs

Challenge	Risk	Reward
Funding	Unable to obtain new resources to support culture of evidence initiatives. Reallocating existing resources has the potential to generate opposition within student affairs and across the institution.	Establishing a culture within student affairs that is outcomes-oriented and data-driven increases the probability that student affairs professionals will be able to: • Work more effectively and efficiently. • Demonstrate the value of what they do. • Grow personally and professionally. • Transform student affairs into a learning organization. • Provide objective data to support funding requests. Reallocating resources demonstrates in a very concrete manner that SSAOs value building a culture of evidence in student affairs and are aware of the opportunity costs associated with current programs and services.
Assessment expertise	Unable to identify a significant number of student affairs professionals with assessment knowledge and skills. This is a possible deal breaker, as assessment is the heart of an effective culture of evidence.	Looking outside student affairs for professionals with assessment expertise creates opportunities for partnerships and buy-in within the institution and across the larger educational community, sends a clear message to student affairs professionals that the endeavor is important, and provides the student affairs team with expert guidance in designing and implementing a culture of evidence.

Competing priorities	Overwhelmed by day-to-day responsibilities that hijack even the best laid plans of vice presidents, deans, directors, and staff. When the president wants a problem resolved *now*, faculty members need updated class rosters yesterday, and transfer students are demanding immediate transcript evaluations, it is difficult to set aside time to design and build a culture of evidence.	Designing and implementing a culture of evidence that leads to data-based decisions places student affairs in a competitive position when it comes to asking for recognition, resources, and support from the institution. Culture of evidence data allow student affairs professionals to clearly demonstrate that the programs and services they offer and the processes they design help the institution to: • Increase student success, persistence, and completion rates. • Fulfill its mission and achieve its goals. • Increase the probability that students will benefit from classroom instruction. • Provide students with opportunities to apply classroom learning to real-life situations. • Acknowledge that the student affairs division is staffed by competent professionals who create conditions that contribute to student and faculty success. • Recognize the value of student affairs.
Building capacity	Encounter resistance from some student affairs professionals who are less than enthusiastic about the mandate to acquire assessment knowledge and skills. Others appear to support the mandate but either find it difficult to set aside the time to participate in professional development activities or have an unrealistic perception of their current skill sets.	Allocating or reallocating funds to build capacity within the student affairs team has a huge payoff. Participating in professional development activities that increase culture of evidence skill sets will help student affairs to: • Strengthen the student affairs team and enable it to compete more effectively for resources. • Improve programs, processes, and services for students and faculty. • Increase each team member's value to the institution and the profession. • Strengthen the image of student affairs across the institution and in the higher education community.
Dealing with fear	"People will discover what I don't know." "I might lose my job." "How can I do this and everything else I am supposed to do?"	Student affairs leaders can reduce fear and anxiety by consistently: • Emphasizing the benefits of building a culture of evidence. • Designing a change process that fits the skill sets of the team. • Creating a climate in which staff members feel valued and safe. • Providing appropriate professional development opportunities. • Sending a clear message that creating a data-based student affairs program is the professionally responsible thing to do.

DEFINITIONS

The following seven definitions offer a common starting point and provide a foundation for this culture of evidence tutorial. Additional definitions appear, as needed, throughout the tutorial.

An ***action plan*** is a sequence of steps that professionals must take to reach a goal. At their most basic, action plans include five elements: (1) a clear statement of the goal, (2) a list of the specific tasks required to reach the goal, (3) identification of the person or group responsible for each task, (4) a time line for each task, and (5) criteria to determine goal achievement.

QUICK TIP

"Building cultures of evidence allows student affairs staff to be more focused and presents increased opportunities to move away from boutique programs serving a few students well to intentionally 'scaling up' services to assist more students." —*Charlene Dukes, president, Prince George's Community College (personal communication, May 23, 2012)*

First published in 1979 and last updated in 2012, the ***CAS Professional Standards for Higher Education*** includes a taxonomy of learning and developmental outcomes for student affairs as well as general and specialty standards for functional areas within student affairs. The *CAS Self-Assessment Guides* (2012) offer new rating scales to provide colleges and universities with tools to assess the effectiveness of programs and services.

The term ***culture of evidence*** refers to a commitment among student affairs professionals to use hard data to show how the programs they offer, the processes they implement, and the services they provide are effective and contribute significantly to an institution's ability to reach its stated goals and fulfill its mission.

Every student affairs division needs a ***mission statement*** that is compatible with the mission statement of the institution and clearly states why student affairs exists, what it does, and how it helps the institution fulfill its mission.

The term ***opportunity costs*** refers to comparing the value of the programs and services student affairs currently offers with the value of the programs and services it could offer if current programs and services were modified or eliminated.

Student affairs describes the administrative unit that houses nonclassroom support services. The term also refers to the body of knowledge, professional literature, and guiding philosophy shared by all who provide nonclassroom support services (Helfgot, 2005).

The term ***student services*** describes programs, services, and activities provided by the division of student affairs. These often include, but are not limited to, academic support, admissions, advising, articulation, assessment, athletics, auxiliary services, career and educational planning, college safety, college survival skills, cooperative education, counseling, financial aid, Greek life, health and wellness, housing, job placement and referral, orientation, outreach and recruitment, records and registration, service learning, student behavior, student life and leadership, and targeted support for specific student populations (e.g., adult learners, e-learners, first-generation-in-college students, international students, and students with disabilities) (Helfgot, 2005).

Student development has two meanings, as the term can refer to both a theory and a goal. As a theory, student development describes how students change, grow, and develop as a result of the college experience. As a goal, the term refers to the commitment of student affairs professionals to provide programs and services that help students develop in positive ways while they are in college (Helfgot, 2005).

MAPPING THE CULTURE OF EVIDENCE JOURNEY

As this tutorial will demonstrate, there is no one-size-fits-all approach to creating a culture of evidence in student affairs. However, mature cultures of evidence share four essential characteristics:

1. They are linked to the institution's mission and culture.
2. They are based on 10 core elements:
    ☼ A student affairs mission statement that is periodically reviewed and updated.
    ☼ A student affairs culture of evidence plan that is periodically reviewed and updated.

IN THE SPOTLIGHT

Kathleen Hetherington, president of Howard Community College in Columbia, Maryland, believes that these five principles should guide culture of evidence initiatives in student affairs:

☼ The culture of evidence in student affairs must be tied to the institution's culture of evidence.

☼ Peer review is essential. Howard Community College, for example, measures performance in all areas against key performance indicators that relate to the college's mission and strategic plan. The president chairs a monthly meeting of a committee composed of representatives from all segments of the college community to examine key performance indicators.

☼ Establishing a robust culture of evidence takes time, but the investment is worth it. A culture of evidence leads to a more focused and fine-tuned institution and increases the accuracy and efficiency with which resources are allocated.

☼ Building a culture of evidence is an ongoing process. Student affairs professionals cannot simply put a culture of evidence in place and walk away. They must continually review data generated by culture of evidence initiatives, make decisions based on the data, and use the data to strengthen programs, policies, procedures, and services.

☼ Student affairs professionals must answer two questions about the programs and services they offer and the procedures they follow: (a) What difference do they make to students and to the college, and (b) how will student affairs professionals demonstrate that they make a difference? (personal communication, April 18, 2012)

- ☼ An annual or semiannual assessment calendar for major areas, programs, and services in student affairs.
- ☼ Programs, services, and activities with clearly defined outcomes (developmental, learning, or program) and outcome measures.
- ☼ Budgeting, planning, and staff development procedures that are data-based, action-oriented, and tied to institutional goals.
- ☼ Formal faculty and student evaluations of programs and services conducted on a regularly scheduled basis.
- ☼ Formal faculty and student needs analyses conducted on a regular basis.
- ☼ Point-of-service assessment activities conducted periodically throughout the year.
- ☼ Research studies to determine the effectiveness of and to improve major initiatives (e.g., courses on life/career planning or college success), solve a problem, or answer a significant question.
- ☼ Data used to drive improvements in programs, processes, and services.

3. They are built on a foundation in student affairs that includes:
   - ☼ Continuous professional development opportunities that help staff implement cultures of evidence and correctly use data.
   - ☼ A requirement for student affairs professionals to set aside time to analyze data, identify appropriate actions to take, and reach data-based decisions.
   - ☼ Clear, consistent strategies to communicate with and educate the college community about the contributions student affairs makes to the institution's mission and bottom line.
   - ☼ An annual report to the college community that uses hard data to show how student affairs programs and services help the institution fulfill its mission and achieve its goals.

4. They involve peer review within student affairs and across the college.
   - ☼ Faculty, staff, and administrators provide feedback via needs analyses, program evaluations, and focus groups.
   - ☼ Student affairs professionals participate in collegewide committees to assess the institution's progress toward key indicators.
   - ☼ Faculty members serve on key culture of evidence committees and task forces in student affairs.
   - ☼ Student affairs professionals continually assess the effectiveness of the assessment measures they use and help their colleagues across the college ask and answer two questions: (1) Are we asking the right questions? (2) Are we using the right indicators?

 QUICK TIP

"Allocate resources to support a significant amount of professional development for student affairs staff in preparation for launching culture of evidence initiatives. Continue to provide professional development opportunities for existing staff and new staff to sustain the culture of evidence effort." —*Paul Dale, president, Paradise Valley Community College (personal communication, April 17, 2012)*

BUILDING CAPACITY

Building capacity in student affairs is one of the most important steps in creating a culture of evidence. It helps professionals recognize their strengths, identify gaps, and develop strategies to acquire or access missing or incomplete expertise. Checking the Foundation: Definitions and Resources (Exercise 1.1) is designed to help student affairs professionals assess their understanding of basic culture of evidence terms, identify sources of assistance within their institutions, and discover support available in their communities. Assessing Readiness to Implement a Culture of Evidence in Student Affairs That Includes Learning Outcomes (Exercise 1.2) invites readers to assess their knowledge of their district or institution, the teaching-learning process, and culture of evidence tools. Both instruments provide the foundation for Module 2: Establishing a Culture of Evidence Foundation and should be completed before beginning that module.

QUICK TIP

"Make creating a culture of evidence a clearly stated performance expectation. Otherwise, the tasks associated with building such a culture will never be completed." —*Paul Dale, president, Paradise Valley Community College (personal communication, April 17, 2012)*

USING THE CULTURE OF EVIDENCE TUTORIAL

Building a Culture of Evidence in Student Affairs: A Guide for Leaders and Practitioners grew out of NASPA's experiences with the Lumina-funded DegreeNow project in West Virginia and feedback from participants in NASPA's annual Assessment and Persistence Conference. Time and time again, student affairs professionals and even leaders said they understood the *why*, but they were having difficulty with the *how*. Specifically, how do SSAOs identify the most effective strategies to:

- ☼ Deal with the fears, the limited skill sets, and lack of knowledge of some staff?
- ☼ Motivate staff members to "up their game" in relation to creating cultures of evidence when there are so many competing demands on their time and talents?
- ☼ Leverage support within the institution and across the community?
- ☼ Justify redirecting resources in these challenging economic times to strengthen culture of evidence initiatives?
- ☼ Design a culture of evidence model that fits their institution's mission, traditions, and culture as well as the skill sets of their staff?
- ☼ Access culture of evidence models at other institutions, study their colleagues' successes, and learn from their mistakes?
- ☼ Use culture of evidence data to drive improvement?

Each of the modules in this tutorial addresses one or more of these questions.

Module 2, written by Marguerite Culp, provides an introduction to essential culture of evidence topics. This module helps student affairs professionals process the self-assessment instruments they completed in Module 1, distinguish between leading and managing, and use a checklist to assess their division's readiness to begin the culture of evidence journey. In addition, the module provides a PowerPoint presentation to introduce culture of evidence topics, offers a variety of follow-up activities, and includes an adaptation for student affairs programs of many of the Classroom Assessment Techniques first developed by Angelo and Cross (1993).

Developed by Katie Busby and Beatriz Gonzalez Robinson, Module 3 helps SSAOs understand what they need to do to prepare the leadership team to conduct a culture of evidence initiative. The module starts with the basics (mission, vision, and values), identifies strategies and provides tools SSAOs can use, and concludes with guidelines for conducting an assessment/audit. The module also covers the importance of assessment champions and offers strategies for dealing with assessment anxiety.

QUICK TIP

"Assign responsibility for building and coordinating the student affairs culture of evidence initiative to a trained professional at the division or system level. For many years, Paradise Valley struggled to establish a culture of evidence without dedicating any resources to the process. This made it difficult to expand and maintain high levels of staff participation. Once student affairs was able to hire a part-time person to support the planning and data collection aspects of program review and the annual learning outcomes assessment processes, the culture of evidence grew much more quickly." —*Paul Dale, president, Paradise Valley Community College (personal communication, April 17, 2012)*

Tisa Mason and Shana Warkentine Meyer collaborate in Module 4 to explore the role of outcomes (developmental, learning, and program) in student affairs, using concrete examples to show how various areas in student affairs—from advising to veterans affairs—weave outcomes into their culture of evidence initiatives. This module offers valuable insights, observations, and advice from higher education leaders who have written on the effective use of assessment and the importance of creating a culture of evidence in student affairs. Finally, the module addresses an essential question: If student affairs professionals focus exclusively on learning outcomes as the centerpiece of their culture of evidence initiative, are they in danger of appearing one-dimensional, of not telling the whole student affairs story, or of sending the wrong message to the institution about who they are and what they do?

In Module 5, Andrew Wall discusses the importance of using different assessment approaches to gather data that are both credible and useful. The module describes practical approaches to designing and implementing action research, traditional research, and program assessment, and gives concrete examples of how different types of institutions use assessment and research results to demonstrate the effectiveness of student affairs programs and services. Most important, the module frames the culture of evidence discussion by reminding student affairs professionals that students deserve the best the profession has to offer. The role of assessment is to help student affairs professionals determine whether they are doing their best work and whether that work is having a positive effect on students and the institution.

In Module 6, Lori Varlotta shares California State University, Sacramento's journey from a culture of good intentions to a culture of evidence in student affairs. Chronicling the first six years of the implementation process, Varlotta offers unvarnished snapshots of the highs and the lows, provides tips for SSAOs, and explains why creating a culture of evidence in student affairs is not only the right thing to do but also the smart thing to do. This module includes a PowerPoint presentation that outlines a seven-step assessment model, provides

QUICK TIP

"Factor program and developmental outcomes into culture of evidence initiatives. Student learning outcomes are part of a culture of evidence; they are not the entire culture of evidence. Integrate outcome data into the institution's larger systems (e.g., program review, personnel evaluations, and new program development)." —*Paul Dale, president, Paradise Valley Community College (personal communication, April 17, 2012)*

numerous examples of how to apply the model, and discusses the use of the workload estimator approach in student affairs.

Module 7, written by Brian Dietz and Kathryn Mueller, examines the important role CAS standards can play in jump-starting and guiding culture of evidence initiatives. It provides a link to a PowerPoint presentation that describes how one institution uses the CAS learning domains in its assessment practices. The module describes strategies student affairs professionals can use to encourage faculty to become more involved in evaluating and shaping support programs and services. Finally, the module reinforces the importance of action research in culture of evidence initiatives, offers action research guidelines and examples from a variety of institutions, and provides an introduction to the program review process.

Marguerite Culp, Gwendolyn Jordan Dungy, and David Jones team up in Module 8 to provide student affairs professionals with tools they can use to assess what they have learned about building cultures of evidence in student affairs, understand the challenges associated with designing and maintaining a culture of evidence, and identify the steps they can take to help their institutions build cultures of evidence in student affairs.

Throughout the tutorial, readers will find sections dedicated to advice from experienced professionals (Quick Tips), concrete examples of how institutions have applied the concepts or used the tools described in the module (In the Spotlight), and exercises to help them assess their knowledge of and ability to apply the concepts introduced in the modules (Apply the Concepts). The tutorial also includes practical tools such as PowerPoint presentations and assessment instruments as well as listings of print and electronic resources.

APPLY THE CONCEPTS

Exercise 1.1—*Checking the Foundation: Definitions and Resources*

Student affairs professionals rarely need to start from scratch to build a culture of evidence, but many do so because they are unaware of the data and resources already available at their institution. Part 1 of this survey asks respondents to identify available institutional data. Part 2 focuses on the support available in the institution, the community, and the higher education world. Part 3 allows respondents to check their knowledge of essential culture of evidence definitions.

PART 1

Directions: Put a check in front of the data currently available at or through your institution. If you are not sure what is available, consult colleagues in the institutional research office, the institutional effectiveness office, and the institutional technology office.

_____ Trend data on prospective students (e.g., ACT, College Board, or National Center for Educational Statistics)

_____ Data from national surveys in which the college has participated (e.g., National Survey of Student Engagement [NSSE], Community College Survey of Student Engagement [CSSE], or Cooperative Institutional Research Program [CIRP])

_____ Data from state-mandated studies or reports

_____ Data generated by or for CAS self-assessment guides

_____ Comparison data that enable colleges to determine how they are doing in major areas compared with peer institutions (Integrated Postsecondary Education Data System [IPEDS])

_____ Student data, such as admissions, financial aid, retention, academic standing, and graduation

_____ Data from locally mandated studies or reports

_____ Other (please identify)

PART 2

Directions: Put a check in front of the assistance available to student affairs professionals as they work toward building a culture of evidence at your institution.

Within the Institution	From Neighboring Institutions, Businesses, and Civic Organizations	Via Professional Organizations
_____ Formal or informal support services provided by the institutional research office, the institutional effectiveness office, or the institutional technology office	_____ Institutional research, institutional effectiveness, or institutional technology professionals who are willing to share their time and talents either in person (e.g., workshops for student affairs staff) or electronically (e.g., Skype or webinars)	_____ Webinars on the topic of implementing a culture of evidence in student affairs— offered by national organizations such as NASPA or ACPA (American College Personnel Association)
_____ Faculty members (current or retired) who have expertise in research methods and statistics	_____ Faculty members in the social sciences, applied mathematics, or business who are willing to design and deliver seminars for student affairs professionals	_____ State and national conferences offered by associations that focus on culture of evidence topics (e.g., NASPA's Assessment and Persistence Conference)
_____ Faculty members (current or retired) who have expertise in building cultures of evidence	_____ Student affairs professionals who have developed cultures of evidence and are willing to share information and serve as mentors	_____ Websites, blogs, and listservs devoted to culture of evidence resources
_____ A collegewide committee whose primary mission is to support culture of evidence initiatives	_____ Websites with culture of evidence information and examples	_____ Electronic and print resources that focus on culture of evidence topics
_____ Graduate students who have assessment and research skills and who might be available for internships or part-time work	_____ Graduate students who have assessment and research skills and who might be available for internships or part-time work	_____ Affinity groups within professional associations that focus on one or more culture of evidence topics

PART 3

Directions: Match each assessment term with the definition that best fits. Write the letter of the definition in the space provided next to each assessment term.

Assessment Terms	Definitions
___1. Culture of evidence	A. "Any effort to gather, analyze and interpret evidence that describes institutional, departmental, divisional, or agency effectiveness" (Upcraft & Schuh, 1996, p. 18)
___2. Curriculum mapping	B. "Any effort to use assessment evidence to improve institutional, department, or agency effectiveness" (Upcraft & Schuh, 1996, p. 19)
___3. Traditional assessment	C. Use of multiple choice, true and false, fill-in-the-blanks, and similar assessments to determine whether students have learned what they were supposed to learn
___4. Authentic assessment	D. Measures learning by asking students to apply the knowledge they have acquired to real-world tasks
___5. Assessment	E. Scoring strategy to measure learning outcomes that lists the criteria evaluators will use to determine the extent to which students have mastered the tasks, skills, or knowledge associated with a program, service, activity, or class
___6. Developmental outcome	F. Determines whether and to what degree students have learned what they were supposed to learn by participating in a student-affairs-sponsored program, service, activity, experience, or class
___7. Program outcome	G. Determines whether student affairs programs, services, activities, experiences, or classes accomplish what they are designed to accomplish
___8. Learning outcome	H. Determines whether and to what degree student behaviors, beliefs, or values change as a result of participation in a student-affairs-sponsored program, service, activity, or class
___9. Rubric	I. A commitment among student affairs professionals to demonstrate, using hard data, how the programs they offer, the processes they implement, and the services they provide are effective and contribute in a significant way to the institution's ability to reach its stated goals and fulfill its mission
___10. Evaluation	J. A process designed to show a clear relationship between the institution's general education outcomes or key performance indicators and specific courses, programs, services, or activities

Answer key on page 19.

APPLY THE CONCEPTS

Exercise 1.2—*Assessing Readiness to Implement a Culture of Evidence in Student Affairs That Includes Learning Outcomes*

Directions: Put a check in the column that best represents your knowledge or skill level in relation to the topic. The skill levels are defined as:

- **Developing:** Limited knowledge or skills but willing to learn.
- **Proficient:** Able to use knowledge/skills to develop programs and services.
- **Exemplary:** Capable of helping others acquire skills and knowledge in this area.

COLLEGE/DISTRICT

Rate your knowledge of the following aspects of your college, university, or district.

	Developing	Proficient	Exemplary
Mission and goals			
Collegewide general education or learning outcomes			
Collegewide plan to assess outcomes			
Planning, resource allocation, and governance structure			
Culture across the college/district			
Culture within student affairs			
Support within student affairs for creating a culture of evidence			
Support across the college/district for creating a culture of evidence in student affairs			

TEACHING AND LEARNING

Rate your knowledge of and ability to apply theories and research related to the following topics.

	Developing	Proficient	Exemplary
Adult development			
Classroom management			
Cognitive development			
Connecting students with out-of-classroom support services			
Designing and implementing partnerships between academic and student affairs			
Engaging students			
Learning styles			
Learning theories			
Student development			
Teaching styles			

ASSESSMENT OF LEARNING

Rate your knowledge of and ability to use the following in helping student affairs implement a culture of evidence that includes learning outcomes.

	Developing	Proficient	Exemplary
Classroom assessment techniques (as outlined by Angelo & Cross, 1993)			
Traditional assessment strategies (e.g., tests and quizzes)			
Authentic assessment strategies (e.g., observations and portfolios)			
Developmental, learning, and program outcomes			
Rubrics			
Nationally standardized instruments			

RESEARCH

Rate your ability to do the following research-related activities.

	Developing	Proficient	Exemplary
Identify a book, a journal, and a website with the potential to help you design and implement a culture of evidence in student affairs			
List the information currently available in your institution's databases that might help student affairs create a culture of evidence			
Explain the difference between action research and research published in peer-reviewed journals			
List the major factors to consider in choosing between purchasing a nationally standardized instrument or developing a local instrument			
Use sampling techniques and web-based survey instruments such as SurveyMonkey, Survey Pro, or PsychData			
Use basic statistical packages such as Excel, SPSS, or SAS			
Explain the strengths, limits, and usefulness of qualitative and quantitative research in student affairs			
Develop protocols and guidelines for the collection, organization, and analysis of data			
Understand and apply basic measurement theory			
Understand and use basic statistical tools			
Identify nationally standardized instruments that might prove useful in implementing a culture of evidence in student affairs			

STUDENT SUCCESS

Rate your overall ability to help student affairs assess the effectiveness of programs and services in the area in which you work (e.g., admissions, counseling, financial aid).

	Developing	Proficient	Exemplary
Area:_____			

RESOURCES

Banta, T. W. (1989–2012). *Assessment update: Progress, trends, and practices in higher education.* San Francisco, CA: Jossey-Bass.

Banta, T. W., Jones, E. A., & Black, K. E. (2009). *Designing effective assessment: Principles and profiles of good practice.* San Francisco, CA: Jossey-Bass.

Brescianni, M. J. (2006). *Outcomes-based academic and co-curricular program review: A compilation of good practice case studies.* Sterling, VA: Stylus.

Keeling, R. P. (Ed.). (2004). *Learning reconsidered: A campus-wide focus on the student experience.* Washington, DC: American College Personnel Association and National Association of Student Personnel Administrators.

Keeling, R. P. (Ed.). (2006). *Learning reconsidered 2: A practical guide to implementing a campus-wide focus on the student experience.* Washington, DC: American College Personnel Association, Association of College and University Housing Officers–International, Association of College Unions International, National Academic Advising Association, National Association for Campus Activities, National Association of Student Personnel Administrators, and National Intramural-Recreational Sports Association.

Keeling, R. P., Wall, A. F., Underhile, R., & Dungy, G. J. (2008). *Assessment reconsidered: Institutional effectiveness for student success.* Washington, DC: National Association of Student Personnel Administrators.

Lock Haven University. (2010). Assessment resources. Retrieved from http://www.lhup.edu/planning-and-assessment/assessment/resources.htm

National Association of Student Personnel Administrators. (2009). International assessment and retention conference presentations. Retrieved from http://www.naspa.org/assessment/presentations.cfm

National Institute for Learning Outcomes Assessment. (2012). Retrieved from http://www.learningoutcomesassessment.org

North Carolina State University. (2012). Internet resources for higher education outcomes assessment. Retrieved from http://www2.acs.ncsu.edu/UPA/assmt/resource.htm

Penn State. (n.d.). Student affairs research and assessment. Retrieved from http://www.sa.psu.edu/SARA/pulse.shtml

Schuh, J. H. (2009). *Assessment methods for student affairs.* San Francisco, CA: Jossey-Bass.

Schuh, J. H., & Upcraft, M. L. (2000). *Assessment practice in student affairs: An applications manual.* San Francisco, CA: Jossey-Bass.

Suskie, L. (2009). *Assessing student learning: A common sense guide.* San Francisco, CA: Jossey-Bass.

Upcraft, M. L., & Schuh, J. H. (1996). *Assessment in student affairs: A guide for practitioners.* San Francisco, CA: Jossey-Bass.

Whitt, E. J. (Ed.). (1999). *Student learning as student affairs work: Responding to our imperative.* Washington, DC: National Association of Student Personnel Administrators.

REFERENCES

American Council on Education. (1937). *The student personnel point of view.* Retrieved from http://myacpa.org/pub/documents/1937.pdf

American Council on Education. (1949). *The student personnel point of view.* Retrieved from http://www.bgsu.edu/colleges/library/cac/sahp/pages/1949SPPVrev.pdf

Angelo, T. A., & Cross, K. P. (1993). *Classroom assessment techniques: A handbook for college teachers.* San Francisco, CA: Jossey-Bass.

Council for the Advancement of Standards in Higher Education (CAS). (2006). *Frameworks for assessing learning and development outcomes.* Washington, DC: Author.

Council for the Advancement of Standards in Higher Education (CAS). (2012). *CAS professional standards for higher education.* Washington, DC: Author.

Council for the Advancement of Standards in Higher Education (CAS). (2012). *CAS self-assessment guides (version 5.0).* Washington, DC: Author.

Culp, M. M. (2012, June). *Evidence-based practices in student affairs.* Program presented at the NASPA Assessment and Persistence Conference, Tampa, FL.

Helfgot, S. R. (2005). Core values and major issues in student affairs practice: What really matters? In S. R. Helfgot & M. M. Culp (Eds.), *community college student affairs: What really matters?* (New directions for community colleges, no. 131, pp. 5-18). San Francisco, CA: Jossey-Bass.

Answer key for Exercise 1.1, Part 3: 1-I, 2-J, 3-C, 4-D, 5-A, 6-H, 7-G, 8-F, 9-E, 10-B

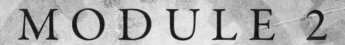

MODULE 2

Establishing a Culture of Evidence Foundation

Marguerite McGann Culp

BUILDING AN EFFECTIVE CULTURE OF EVIDENCE presents a challenge to even the most experienced student affairs professionals. This module offers a brief introduction to essential topics that Modules 3 through 7 will explore in depth. In addition to helping student affairs professionals use the tools introduced in Module 1 to evaluate and strengthen their culture of evidence skill sets, Module 2 includes a checklist to help professionals determine the strength of student affairs at their institution, guidelines for leading and managing the transition from a culture of good intentions to a culture of evidence, and practical tips from presidents and higher education leaders. The module also includes a PowerPoint presentation on basic culture of evidence concepts.

USING DATA TO ESTABLISH A BASELINE AND STRENGTHEN THE TEAM

Establishing a culture of evidence baseline begins with analyzing responses to the self-assessment exercises in Module 1. Responses to Parts 1 and 2 of Checking the Foundation: Definitions and Resources (see Exercise 1.1 on p. 11) identify what student affairs professionals know about the availability of data and resources in the college and across the community, while Part 3 establishes what they know about basic culture of evidence terms. Responses to the Assessing Readiness to Implement a Culture

QUICK TIP

"The leadership in student affairs has to *lead*. They must develop a vision based on institutional priorities and link all programs, services, and initiatives to that vision, setting metrics and benchmarks along the way. Student affairs professionals cannot be insular in their thinking. They need to know about best practices and promising practices; they must be more focused and meaningful in taking risks to do the right things for students—for the right reasons." —*Charlene Dukes, president, Prince George's Community College (personal communication, May 23, 2012)*

of Evidence in Student Affairs That Includes Learning Outcomes (see Exercise 1.2 on p. 14), help professionals recognize what they know and what they need to learn about their institution or district, the teaching-learning process, and assessment and research tools.

THE STUDENT AFFAIRS LEADERSHIP TEAM

Using baseline data to strengthen the skill sets of individual student affairs professionals, specific areas within student affairs, and the team at the top is a fairly straightforward process that involves helping everyone recognize their strengths, identify important gaps, and develop plans to build on the strengths and close the gaps. Timing and focus are crucial—even well-thought-out plans will fail if the capacity or focus required to execute them is lacking.

It is essential that members of the student affairs leadership team understand the importance of managing as well as leading. Table 2.1 provides an overview of strategies for effectively leading and managing culture of evidence initiatives.

Table 2.1

Strategies to Help the Student Affairs Leadership Team Build a Culture of Evidence

	Leading	Managing
Budgeting	Make culture of evidence initiatives one of the cornerstones of the budget-building process. Set aside "opportunity money" from the annual budget to support culture of evidence activities during the year.	Build a system to monitor compliance with timelines and mandates that relate to culture of evidence initiatives in the budget-building process. Establish procedures for staff to follow to access opportunity money.
Communication	Communicate the importance of creating a culture of evidence in student affairs in a clear, positive, and unambiguous manner. Communication starts in student affairs and continues across the entire educational community, including the board of trustees.	Periodically verify that the college community is hearing a consistent message from the student affairs team about the importance of and need for a culture of evidence in student affairs.

Focus	Keep the spotlight on culture of evidence initiatives by: • Funding onsite professional development opportunities. • Helping student affairs professionals follow the data, even when the results inconvenience or disappoint some members of the team. • Asking the essential questions: (a) how does each student affairs program, process, or service help the institution fulfill its mission; and (b) how will student affairs demonstrate this to the institution using hard data?	Implement a professional development series for all student affairs staff that addresses key culture of evidence topics: • Data available at the institution. • Resources available in the institution and across the community. • Designing cultures of evidence: learning from student affairs colleagues across the country. • Implementing and assessing outcomes (developmental, learning, and program) in student affairs. • Assessment strategies for student affairs. • Action research: when and how to use it.
Morale and motivation	Understand that leadership matters, especially when asking staff to build a culture of evidence in student affairs. Keep every area in student affairs moving in the right direction. • Celebrate successes. • Learn from failures. • Communicate clearly that building a culture of evidence does not happen overnight.	Build confidence by: • Helping staff members identify and build on existing strengths. • Pilot-testing culture of evidence initiatives in strong programs and services. • Providing multiple opportunities for staff members to acquire the knowledge and skills they need to build a culture of evidence in student affairs.
Planning	Shape the culture of evidence vision in student affairs. Focus on empowering staff and removing barriers. Remind everyone that all areas in an institution are involved in supporting, facilitating, or stimulating learning.	Develop an action plan for building a culture of evidence in student affairs. At a minimum, the action plan should include: • Goals. • Specific tasks required to reach each goal. • Clear responsibility and timeline for each task. • Criteria to determine goal achievement. • Strategies to use in communicating results within student affairs and across the institution. • Strategies student affairs will follow in using results to shape programs, processes, and services.
Resources	Establish direction by indicating that building a culture of evidence is a major priority. Help everyone understand why building a culture of evidence in student affairs is important and how their contributions matter. Allocate or reallocate resources to support culture of evidence initiatives.	Organize people, equipment, space, and budgets to support building a culture of evidence in student affairs. Create systems to encourage student affairs staff members to design and implement a culture of evidence throughout the division.

Results	Help student affairs professionals learn by constantly exposing them to assessment data and asking them what they learned from the data.	Establish a uniform reporting format for all culture of evidence activities.
	Link culture of evidence data to major initiatives in student affairs; for example, budget building, resource allocation (people, space, and money), and strategic planning.	Provide training and tools to help student affairs professionals use the uniform reporting format.
	Share culture of evidence results with the college community.	Require major areas in student affairs to schedule time to analyze culture of evidence data and develop data-based recommendations to improve programs and services.
Structure	Build effective working relationships with key players within student affairs, across the institution, and in the community including: • Student affairs leaders, midlevel managers, and key people in specific areas • Board of trustees • President • Cabinet members • Faculty senate • Institutional Technology, Institutional Research, Institutional Effectiveness • Faculty leaders • Community leaders	Assess the institutional climate. Provide the student affairs leadership team with practical assistance in designing culture of evidence initiatives consistent with the climate. Schedule a review of the mission, vision, goals, strategic objectives, and performance indicators adopted by the student affairs division to verify that each is consistent with those of the institution. Schedule formal reviews of student affairs programs and services. Appoint process improvement teams that include academic faculty, staff, and administrators to review major processes in student affairs that affect the entire institution (e.g., admissions, records, registration, and financial aid). Monitor implementation of the culture of evidence action plan for student affairs.

QUICK TIP

"Require the student affairs team to set aside a specific number of hours each month to analyze data. Everyday tasks will consume the team's time unless data collection and analysis become part of the culture." —*John R. Laws, vice chancellor for student affairs, Ivy Tech Community College (personal communication, May 11, 2012)*

It also is essential for leaders to establish a culture of evidence baseline for the student affairs team. Constructing that baseline starts with using the two self-assessment instruments in Module 1 (Checking the Foundation: Definitions and Resources; and Assessing Readiness to Implement a Culture of Evidence in Student Affairs That Includes Learning Outcomes) to help team members develop an accurate picture of their strengths and weaknesses. This picture will help student affairs leaders:

1. Recognize and build on areas in student affairs that already have culture of evidence elements in place.
2. Identify gaps that matter.
3. Develop a plan to build on the team's strengths, minimize its weaknesses, and deal with gaps that have the potential to weaken culture of evidence initiatives.

4. Link developing and working the plan to each staff member's annuals goals and performance review.

5. Provide a variety of opportunities for student affairs professionals to implement their professional development plan. Arrange in-service training, invite consultants to campus, organize study groups, and support participation in webinars and state or national conferences.

6. Identify key players across the institution who are capable of and willing to assist student affairs professionals in designing and implementing an effective culture of evidence.

QUICK TIP

"[The idea of] . . . using real data to drive decisions is appealing; interest in the activities required to develop good information is often lower. Using an incremental approach that focuses on achievable goals helps mitigate concerns about the time required to implement a culture of evidence." —*Sarah Westfall, vice president for student development and dean of students, Kalamazoo College (personal communication, May 24, 2012)*

7. Involve these key players in helping student affairs design and implement a culture of evidence by asking them to:

   a. Provide professional development activities (e.g., how to design and implement action plans, outcomes, rubrics, and assessment strategies).

   b. Help student affairs professionals identify and access institutional resources (e.g., available assessment data or information technology support).

   c. Teach student affairs professionals how to map student learning that results from programs and services provided by student affairs to the institution's general education outcomes.

   d. Review culture of evidence products as they evolve (e.g., action plans, outcomes, rubrics, assessment strategies, and assessment results).

   e. Mentor or serve as resources to student affairs staff members throughout the implementation process.

8. Develop an initial culture of evidence plan that is realistic and leverages the skills and resources available in the student affairs division.

9. Tie the culture of evidence plan to the institution's culture of evidence plan and to the budgeting and resource allocation process in student affairs.

10. Pilot test and refine the culture of evidence plan.

STUDENT AFFAIRS PROFESSIONALS

In addition to honestly assessing their strengths and identifying what they need to learn, student affairs professionals must build on strengths, focus on the gaps that matter, and demonstrate that they are able to:

1. Understand the mission, goals, and culture of the institution in which they work.

2. Identify their strengths and weaknesses in relation to building a culture of evidence in student affairs, and accept the fact that building such a culture starts with them.

3. Design a plan to build on their strengths, minimize their weaknesses, and close any gap that has the potential to weaken their ability to understand or contribute to culture of evidence initiatives. Such a plan must become part of each staff member's annual goals and annual performance review.

4. Seek out and participate in professional development activities at their institution, across the state, and around the country, then share what they learn with their colleagues.

5. Collect examples of strong culture of evidence practices and models in their area of responsibility.

IN THE SPOTLIGHT

John R. Laws, vice chancellor for student affairs at Ivy Tech Community College in Indiana, considers the following five principles essential for senior student affairs officers based on his experience creating a culture of evidence at a multicampus institution:

- Encourage everyone on the student affairs team to build capacity by participating in professional development activities designed to increase culture of evidence skill sets.

- Articulate two expectations: (1) the student affairs leadership team will schedule staff meetings to review data and analyze how to use the data to strengthen programs, services, policies, and procedures; and (2) end-of-year reports will be based on data and evidence.

- Create a positive working relationship with the Institutional Research Office. Someone who understands how to extract reports from the current system and how to make sense of the data can save you hours of time searching for trends and patterns.

- Do not view data in isolation. Look at multiple reports. Search for trends and patterns within campuses and across the system.

- Take the time and do the work to create a real culture of evidence. Building a culture of evidence sounds good, but too often student affairs professionals are not able or willing to put in the time or the effort to create a culture that lasts. (personal communication, May 11, 2012)

6. Read, surf the Internet, and join e-mail lists devoted to culture of evidence topics in their area of responsibility.

7. Consider organizing or joining a study group in their area of expertise that focuses on specific culture of evidence topics.

8. Spend a day or two shadowing professionals at institutions with robust cultures of evidence in the area in which they work.

9. Actively participate in designing, pilot testing, and refining the culture of evidence model for student affairs. Make sure that the plan is realistic and builds on the skills and resources available in the student affairs division.

10. Communicate with their colleagues in student affairs and across the institution in a positive, data-based manner about the importance of establishing a culture of evidence in student affairs and how such a culture will strengthen the institution's ability to fulfill its mission and achieve its goals—and increase the ability of student affairs to compete for institutional, state, and national funding

Quick Tip

"Do not try to replicate what another college is doing without determining if the college's approach fits the culture, skill sets, and resources of your institution. Do not purchase a piece of software without having a plan and a clear understanding of how the software fits into that plan. Do not underestimate the time and energy required to design, implement, and maintain a culture of evidence. Never create an atmosphere where student affairs professionals feel inadequate because of what they do not know about building a culture of evidence."

—*William E. Carter, vice chancellor, information technology, Houston Community College System (personal communication, May 9, 2012)*

Learning More About Culture of Evidence Topics

Building a Culture of Evidence in Student Affairs: Establishing a Baseline (available at http://www.naspa.org/cultureofevidence/MOD2PP.pdf) is an interactive presentation that takes 60–90 minutes to complete. Exercises that supplement the presentation can be found at the end of this module and are labeled as follows:

✿ Exercise 2.1—Follow-up Activities for the Presentation "Building a Culture of Evidence in Student Affairs: Establishing a Baseline"

✿ Exercise 2.2—Assessing Student Affairs at Your Institution

✿ Exercise 2.3— Classroom Assessment Techniques (CATs) That Are Useful in Student Affairs

✿ Exercise 2.4—Snapshot of Traditional and Authentic Assessment Tools Used in Student Affairs

It is important for student affairs professionals to follow up on the presentation, either individually or in groups. An institution's culture, the goals of the senior student affairs officer, and the skill sets of student affairs professionals determine which follow-up activities will work best in a specific setting.

APPLY THE CONCEPTS

Exercise 2.1—*Follow-up Activities for the Presentation Building a Culture of Evidence in Student Affairs: Establishing a Baseline*

1. **Create a professional development plan.** Identify the skills and knowledge you need to acquire to contribute to student affairs' efforts to build an effective culture of evidence. Develop an action plan to acquire these skills.

   Goals:

   ⚙ Establish a realistic picture of your skill sets and knowledge base.
   ⚙ Identify gaps that matter.
   ⚙ Develop a clear plan for reducing these gaps.

2. **Develop a portfolio.** Show how your area currently measures and demonstrates the effectiveness of the programs and services it offers. Share the portfolio with other areas within student affairs and ask your colleagues to (1) identify the strengths and weaknesses of your portfolio, and (2) suggest strategies to strengthen the ways in which your area demonstrates the effectiveness of its programs and services.

   Goals:

   ⚙ Establish a clear culture of evidence baseline for each area in student affairs.
   ⚙ Enhance collaboration and cooperation among student affairs professionals.
   ⚙ Expand what student affairs professionals know about areas other than their own.

3. **Review the CAS standards.** List the elements of the standards for the area in which you work that might prove useful in demonstrating the effectiveness of programs and services.

   Goal:

   ⚙ Increase ability to incorporate CAS standards into culture of evidence initiatives.

4. **Search the Internet.** Locate three institutions that appear to have strong cultures of evidence in student affairs. Evaluate the cultures of evidence. Identify three elements of the cultures of evidence that might work at your institution.

   Goal:

   ⚙ Increase ability to identify and learn from similar institutions with cultures of evidence in place in student affairs.

5. **Synthesize the information.** Reflect on what you have learned from the CAS standards, the Internet search, and the input on your portfolio offered by colleagues. Update your area's portfolio by including a list of the changes you would like to make in your area's approach to demonstrating the effectiveness of the programs and services it offers. Share your portfolio with colleagues and incorporate their feedback into your final product.

Goals:

- ✿ Increase ability to analyze, evaluate, and apply information.
- ✿ Enhance collaboration and cooperation among student affairs professionals.
- ✿ Expand what student affairs professionals know about areas other than their own.

6. **Develop templates.** Collaborate with your colleagues to develop guidelines for student affairs professionals to follow in designing and implementing a culture of evidence in student affairs.

Goal:

- ✿ Increase consistency within student affairs by adopting divisionwide guidelines.

Quick Tip

"Consider establishing a Data and Decisions Group in concert with academic affairs colleagues; task the group with mining existing data. At Kalamazoo College, this approach built some real competence and familiarity with both data and ways to ask interesting and relevant (to both academic and student affairs staff) questions." —*Sarah Westfall, vice president for student development and dean of students, Kalamazoo College (personal communication, May 24, 2012)*

APPLY THE CONCEPTS

Exercise 2.2—*Assessing Student Affairs at Your Institution*

Directions: Check all the statements that describe student affairs at your institution, then total your responses.

———— Has a mission statement that reflects the institution's mission and core values.

———— Follows planning and evaluation procedures that are clearly defined and understood by the college or university community.

———— Can demonstrate a clear relationship between student affairs policies, programs, and practices and the institution's mission and values.

———— Can demonstrate a clear link between theories and research and student affairs policies, programs, and practices.

———— Can demonstrate *with hard data* that programs and services are based on documented student, faculty, and institutional needs.

———— Can demonstrate *with hard data* that student affairs policies, programs, and practices contribute to student learning.

———— Can demonstrate *with hard data* that student affairs policies, programs, and practices contribute to student success.

———— Provides new staff members with up-to-date job descriptions, an orientation to the institution and to their area of responsibility, and a clear explanation of the institution's expectations.

———— Provides all staff members with opportunities to upgrade their skills.

———— Provides all staff members with the opportunity to meet with supervisors to set annual goals that clearly relate to institutional goals.

———— Evaluates staff members each year. A significant part of the evaluation is based on their ability to achieve annual goals.

———— Offers staff members the opportunity to participate in and influence decisions regarding hiring, the allocation of resources, and the development of goals and outcome measures within student affairs.

———— Communicates with the college or university community effectively and in a timely manner.

———— Provides the college or university community with opportunities to evaluate programs and services designed and implemented by student affairs.

Total Number of Checks

Scoring	
Total checks	**Implications**
11–14	A fairly strong program with a clear understanding of and ability to design and deliver support services that matter to the college's bottom line: student access and success.
6–10	An average program with some understanding of and ability to design and deliver support services that matter to the college's bottom line: student access and success.
1–5	An underdeveloped program that needs to strengthen its understanding of and ability to design and deliver support services that matter to the college's bottom line: student access and success.

Note. Adapted from *Community College Student Affairs: What Really Matters?* (pp. 77–87), by S. R. Helfgot and M. M. Culp (Eds.), 2005, San Francisco, CA: Jossey-Bass. Copyright 2005 by Jossey-Bass. Adapted with permission.

QUICK TIP

"The bottom line for higher education right now is efficiency on investment. Student affairs must demonstrate to the college community that the money allocated to it either generates or saves revenue for the institution. It also must demonstrate that new programs and services are creating efficiencies or are cost-neutral." —*William E. Carter, vice chancellor, information technology, Houston Community College System (personal communication, May 9, 2012)*

APPLY THE CONCEPTS

Exercise 2.3—*Classroom Assessment Techniques (CATs) That Are Useful in Student Affairs*

This list of techniques is adapted from *Classroom Assessment Techniques: A Handbook for College Teachers* by T. A. Angelo and K. P. Cross (1993). The page numbers on which each technique can be found in the original source are provided in parentheses.

- **Background Knowledge Probe:** Use at the start of a class or activity to assess what students already know and to focus their attention. May take the form of a short survey or a few open-ended questions. (p. 121)

- **Focused Listening:** Use before, after, or during an activity or class to assess what students remember about a specific subject or concept. This approach has many variations, but all start with asking students to list the important words or phrases related to a topic in a limited amount of time. (p. 126)

- **Empty Outline:** Use to determine whether students understand the most important points of a presentation, a discussion, a class, or an activity. Present participants with an empty or partially completed outline and give them a short amount of time to fill in the blanks. (p. 138)

- **Memory Matrix:** Use to verify that students can recall important points/concepts in a presentation, discussion, class, or activity. Present participants with a rectangle divided into rows and columns. Provide row and column headings but leave the boxes empty. Ask students to fill in the boxes. (p. 142)

- **Minute Paper:** Use to help students evaluate and apply what they have learned. Stop the presentation, discussion, class, or activity a few minutes early. Ask students to answer two questions: What was the most important thing you learned today? What important question remains unanswered? (p. 148)

- **Muddiest Point:** Use during or at the end of a class, activity, presentation, or discussion to find out what remains unclear or confusing to participants. Simply ask students to write down their answer to one question: What was the muddiest point in _____? (p. 154)

- **Categorizing Grid:** Use to help students think about and organize what they have been learning and to provide student affairs professionals with insight into their students' thought processes. Select two or three important categories. Draw a large rectangle and divide it into columns. Label each column with a key word, phrase, or sentence. Provide students with a list of words or phrases, and ask them to place the words in the correct column. (p. 160)

- **Analytic Memos:** Use to assess how well students can analyze a problem and communicate their analysis clearly and concisely. Present a scenario and ask the students to analyze it and make recommendations regarding appropriate responses. (p. 177)

- **One Sentence Summary:** Use to determine how well students can summarize a large amount of information on a specific topic. Useful for small and large group activities, workshops, and classes. (p. 183)

- **Annotated Portfolios:** Use to determine whether students can apply what they have learned to real-life situations and whether they can connect what they have learned over a series of workshops, classes, or activities. Ask students to prepare a portfolio on a specific topic, as well as a narrative explaining why they chose the elements included in the portfolio. (p. 208)

☼ **Application Cards:** Use to determine whether students can apply what they have learned. After a discussion, group, program, or activity, distribute 3 in. x 5 in. cards to participants and ask them to write down one way they could apply what they have learned in the real world. (p. 236)

☼ **Everyday Ethical Dilemmas:** Use to determine whether students can use what they are learning to solve ethical dilemmas. Develop a case study. Ask students to read the case study and write brief, anonymous responses. (p. 271)

☼ **Interest/Knowledge/Skills Checklists:** Use to help students assess their knowledge and skills at the beginning and end of an experience or activity. Use the results to help students understand what they have learned. Create a checklist of topics and skills related to the program or activity. Ask students to indicate their interest in and assess their knowledge of specific topics. (p. 285)

☼ **Productive Study Time Logs:** Use to help students strengthen their study and time management skills. Create a log for students to complete that will yield important information about how much time they spend studying, when they study, where they study, with whom they study, and how much they multitask while studying. (p. 300)

☼ **Punctuated Lectures/Groups:** Use to focus students' attention on their readiness to benefit from and fully participate in an activity, program, or workshop. Stop the activity, program, or workshop and ask students to simply think about what they were doing during the event and how their behavior increased or decreased the chances they would benefit from the experience. After allowing them to reflect, ask them to summarize their reflections in writing (index card) or electronically (text message). (p. 303)

☼ **Process Analysis:** Use to help students reflect on how they approach their work. Ask them to keep a record of how they approach a specific assignment. Periodically, ask students to reflect on the processes they use in carrying out a specific assignment, separate effective from ineffective processes, and identify process improvement strategies. (p. 307)

Note. Adapted from *Classroom Assessment Techniques: A Handbook for College Teachers* (pp. 121–307), by T. A. Angelo and K. P. Cross, 1993, San Francisco, CA: Jossey-Bass. Copyright 1993 by Jossey-Bass. Adapted with permission.

QUICK TIP

"Student affairs professionals must become the experts on out-of-classroom student learning; continually review programs, services, and processes to determine what they add to student learning; and document in a clear, concise, and easy-to-understand manner the role student affairs plays in learning."
—*Diana Doyle, president, Arapahoe Community College (personal communication, March 11, 2012)*

APPLY THE CONCEPTS

Exercise 2.4—*Snapshot of Traditional and Authentic Assessment Tools Used in Student Affairs*

An effective culture of evidence blends traditional and authentic assessment tools.

Traditional (Frequently Used)	Authentic (Emerging)
Licensing exams	Case studies
National surveys of student satisfaction, beliefs, habits, etc. (e.g., National Survey of Student Engagement [NSSE], Community College Survey of Student Engagement [CSSE], or Cooperative Institutional Research Program [CIRP] Freshman Survey conducted by UCLA)	Capstone experience
Needs assessment	Demonstration
Placement exams	Exit interview
Satisfaction surveys (local)	Focus group
State surveys of self-reported student behaviors (e.g., Core Alcohol and Drug Survey in Illinois)	Journal or diary
State exit exams	Observation
Tests and quizzes	Performance

Note. Most authentic assessment instruments are used with rubrics, a topic that is discussed in Module 4.

MODULE 3

Developing the Leadership Team to Establish and Maintain a Culture of Evidence in Student Affairs

Katie Busby and Beatriz Gonzalez Robinson

THIS MODULE IS GEARED TOWARD demystifying institutional effectiveness practices for senior student affairs officers (SSAOs) and helping them build the capacity of student affairs team leaders to establish and maintain a pervasive culture of evidence. A culture of evidence is crucial to support the work of student affairs professionals in offering programs and services that truly advance student learning and development.

For some student affairs leaders, the term *culture of evidence* might conjure up images of an Orwellian environment in which the aim is surveillance and control. They may wonder how such a culture will view effort and process. They may doubt that the impact of the work they do—with its emphasis on developing the whole person—can be quantified. Some may fear that a culture of evidence will lay bare their department's problems without any assurance that appropriate resources will be applied to ameliorate these problems. Others may think that while it is a good idea to have a clear sense of team progress and student growth, there is not enough time to develop an evaluation framework and stick to it. Maintaining a culture of evidence may seem like too much work with too little (if any) payoff.

If any of this sounds familiar, you are not alone. Anyone who has served on peer-review accreditation teams can tell you about the apprehension and grudging acceptance that surround culture of evidence efforts on many college campuses. Some of the terms used in this arena sound stilted:

QUICK TIP

Remember, your team members are at different points in their knowledge and appreciation of a culture of evidence. Take time to teach your team. Refer to culture of evidence principles not only as part of an annual review but also as opportunities arise, such as when making in-year program adjustments, hiring staff, or reconfiguring student spaces.

culture of evidence, culture of assessment, institutional effectiveness, and *continuous quality improvement.* The whole concept might seem like fodder for management theory wonks, with little application to the day-to-day work of student affairs or, for that matter, to the college. We in higher education are guilty of promulgating some of the pessimism and murkiness that surround the idea of adopting a culture of evidence (Dooris, 2003) by emphasizing jargon and evaluation cycle schematics over the practical and beneficial aspects of such an environment. If student affairs leaders can focus their efforts not only on the necessary details of conducting assessment but also on the broader benefits of examining programs and services with student learning and development in mind, a culture of evidence can develop. Such a culture promotes staff effectiveness—and thus student learning—through the ongoing review of new data presented against identified student outcomes. Thomas Angelo (1999) reminded higher education professionals that "assessment techniques are of little use unless and until local academic cultures value self-examination, reflection, and continuous improvement" (p. 5).

USING THIS MODULE

This module provides SSAOs with information that will enhance their understanding of a culture of evidence in student affairs and empower them to build such a culture at their institution. Aspiring SSAOs and other student affairs professionals should also find the information presented in this module helpful. Specifically, the module:

- ✿ Defines culture of evidence and related terms.
- ✿ Outlines key components in a culture of evidence.
- ✿ Describes strategies that can be used to create a culture of evidence.
- ✿ Includes resources and examples of best practices from different institution types.
- ✿ Quotes SSAOs who are promoting a culture of evidence on their campuses.
- ✿ Provides practical exercises that can be used to promote a culture of evidence.

DEFINITIONS

A culture has a common language; it allows the members to communicate and work well together. To maintain a culture of evidence, student affairs departments should have a working understanding of basic definitions and acknowledged standards that support a focus on proven student learning resulting from interaction with student affairs. Banta (2004) defined a culture of evidence as "an environment in which important decisions are based on the study of relevant data" (p. 6). The terms *culture of assessment* and *culture of evidence* are often used interchangeably; however, the former focuses narrowly on using assessment of student learning, while the latter includes the examination of multiple sources of data and inquiry (TLT Group, n.d.). *Institutional effectiveness*, a term associated with planning and evaluation, is the systematic, ongoing process of gathering and analyzing data to evaluate performance in relation to the mission and goals of the institution. Institutional effectiveness includes the evaluation of academic and administrative units as

well as support services (Head, 2011). Institutional effectiveness focuses on campuswide performance and its effect on mission fulfillment. Exercise 3.3—What Do You Mean By...? is a useful tool to help student affairs staff develop a common language that can be used to build a culture of evidence.

In a culture of evidence—in which information is regularly collected for making decisions, including the commitment of resources—certain components are typically present. These components enable the culture to operate with an internal discipline focused on explicit intentions and actual outcomes.

Components in a culture of evidence include the following elements with which all team members, particularly team leaders, should be familiar. *Core values* are the basic principles or standards that form attitudes and guide behavior. They are the basis for the *mission statement*, which describes to both internal and external stakeholders what you do. The work of a student affairs department of a college or university should flow from the institutional principles and purpose. The mission of the student affairs department should be a reflection of the institution's core values and mission. If you function in an institution that has not articulated its core values, you can glean them from the mission statement and certainly from the ethos of the institution, then work to create or update your student affairs mission statement to be congruent. As part of a larger system, your mission must align with that of the institution for your work to be valued and resourced and for your efforts to have maximum effectiveness. Similarly, units within the student affairs department should develop mission statements that clearly define their role in the system and let students and others know how the unit can help them with their development and experience at the institution. Exercise 3.1—Reflection Questions for Developing Your Mission and Vision can be used by divisions developing or examining their mission and vision statements.

With a strong, shared foundation of core values and mission, student affairs can develop a *vision* that aligns with the institutional and departmental purpose. Jim Collins (2000), author of *Good to Great*, defined vision in the following way:

> Vision is simply a combination of three basic elements: (1) an organization's fundamental reason for existence beyond just making money (often called its mission or purpose); (2) its timeless, unchanging core values; and (3) huge and audacious—but ultimately achievable—aspirations for its own future. (I like to call these BHAGs, or Big Hairy Audacious Goals). (para. 3)

A vision statement is an aspirational description that inspires both daily work and long-term strategic decisions. It focuses on the future and tells everyone what you want to be. Your vision is your doable dream.

With an inspiring endpoint in mind, student affairs team members can develop *goals,* or desired results, to realize their vision for the department and for student development. Student affairs should emulate the institution by developing a strategic plan with long-range and mid-range goals and benchmarks (targets) that guide decisions and actions. A student affairs team inculcated in a culture of evidence maintains an *action plan* that does for the department what the strategic plan does for the institution: provides a road map with a clear destination, route, mile markers, and trip duration. As outlined in Module 1, action plans typically include: (1) a clear statement of the goal, (2) a list of the specific tasks required to reach the goal, (3) the identification of the person or group responsible for each task, (4) a timeline for each task, and (5) criteria to determine goal achievement. Following an action plan format will enable the student affairs team to set SMART goals that are:

- ✿ *Specific* with respect to both the goals themselves and the tasks required for their attainment;
- ✿ *Measurable* in terms of criteria and assessment method;
- ✿ *Assignable,* so responsibility for shepherding the goal does not fall through the cracks;
- ✿ *Resource-conscious* to enable realistic and institution-aligned planning; and
- ✿ *Time-limited,* with time restrictions for task and goal completion.

Your team members might believe they are ready to develop an action plan after having reflected on and articulated a mission and vision, but it is important to take time to scan the environment in which the action plan will be executed. Scanning the internal and external environment to assess your situation and that of your students is critically important. Taking time for this step is particularly important for institutions in which assessment—"the process of defining, selecting, designing, collecting, analyzing, interpreting, and using information to increase students' learning and development" (Erwin, 1991, p. 15)—has been mostly absent. Whether it is an environmental scan, annual evaluation of programs, or assessment of student learning, student affairs can use data already captured by the institution in the form of responses to nationally standardized surveys (e.g., the National Survey of Student Engagement [NSSE] or the National Survey of First-Year Seminars) and internally developed instruments (e.g., graduating student and alumni surveys).

Boone and Kurtz (1995) created a straightforward model for situational analysis that focuses on strengths, weaknesses, opportunities, and threats—a SWOT analysis. Strengths and weaknesses are internal to the institution or department, whereas opportunities and

QUICK TIP

When it comes to goals, remember the following:

- ✿ Goals in student affairs should be linked to the goals listed in the institution's strategic plan, enabling partnerships across the institution and providing a compelling rationale for the allocation of resources.

- ✿ Goals are sometimes referred to as objectives or planning priorities. Don't get hung up on the labels; focus on a common understanding of the terms to be used in your own culture of evidence.

- ✿ Goals can be geared toward improved functioning of the student affairs department or improved or acquired behaviors, knowledge, and skills of students (student learning outcomes [SLOs]).

threats are external. The SWOT framework guides goal setting by directing analysis toward matching elements of the SWOT results:

✿ Strength + Opportunity = Leverage point (maximize your existing advantages)
✿ Weakness + Opportunity = Constraint (address what is restraining growth)
✿ Strength + Threat = Vulnerability (keep tabs on areas susceptible to negative trends)
✿ Weakness + Threat = Problem (fortify deficient areas to avoid further negative impact)

Foundations

Besides the preliminary work of reviewing the student affairs mission and vision and conducting a situational analysis, teams should steep themselves in the standards and generally desired student learning and development outcomes upheld by their professional organizations. The following summary of primary standards and desired student outcomes is geared toward the work of student affairs professionals. These works should be required reading in the department and should be used to inform goals.

CAS Professional Standards for Higher Education. For more than 30 years, the Council for the Advancement of Standards in Higher Education (CAS) has promoted standards that foster sound professional practice and student development. These standards are criteria and principles for assessing and improving programs and services. The *CAS Professional Standards for Higher Education* (2012) provides standards for more than 40 functional areas in student support services, such as advising and campus activities; commuter and multicultural programs; and career, counseling, clinical health, dining, and disability services. Each of the CAS standards has multiple subsections (covering, for example, mission, leadership, and resources) for which CAS publishes *Self-Assessment Guides* (SAGs) that help teams identify strengths and weakness in functional areas. CAS standards, which also include 16 student learning domains, are additionally supported by *Frameworks for Assessing Learning and Development Outcomes* (FALDOs). Thus, a SAG is a tool for assessing programs, while a FALDO is used to assess student learning in relation to CAS standards. The results of assessments using SAGs and FALDOs can supply ample data for internal elements of a SWOT analysis.

Learning Reconsidered. The publication *Learning Reconsidered: A Campus-Wide Focus on the Student Experience* (Keeling, 2004) examined and questioned conventional organizational structures in academe vis-à-vis student learning and development, with a particular focus on the effect of the student affairs department on student outcomes. The booklet was followed by *Learning Reconsidered 2: A Practical Guide to Implementing a Campus-Wide Focus on the Student Experience* (Keeling, 2006), which explored how educators across the campus can use all institutional resources to teach and develop the whole student. This report described the experiences of student affairs professionals who had explicitly linked their programs and services to expected student learning outcomes and had assessed those outcomes. Both publications contain seven broad student outcomes, which an institution or department can use to develop more specific learning outcomes.

CAS Learning and Developmental Outcomes. In 2008—in light of the publication of the *Learning Reconsidered* books—CAS revisited the 16 learning domains included in its standards and integrated the CAS learning outcomes with the outcomes in *Learning Reconsidered*. The resulting document contains 6 student outcome domains and 28 outcome domain dimensions. Compliance with CAS standards requires student affairs functional units to identify and assess student learning outcomes associated with the six domains. The domains and related dimensions provide a streamlined framework for developing program goals and student learning outcomes as part of a culture of evidence.

Professional Competency Areas for Student Affairs Practitioners. Working together to advance professional growth and development in higher education student affairs, ACPA–College Student Educators International and NASPA–Student Affairs Administrators in Higher Education (2010) published a document listing the expected knowledge, skills, and attitudes for those working in the field, regardless of specialization. Besides setting the basis for professional development in student affairs, this document provides benchmarks for individual and team growth and assessment in a culture of evidence.

DEVELOPING A CULTURE OF EVIDENCE

Developing a culture of evidence can be a very challenging yet rewarding endeavor. It requires a strong commitment from an SSAO who values the use of credible data in decision making. Other key components are a divisionwide vision and mission, and SMART goals linked to the institutional mission and priorities. SWOT analyses and existing data, as well as peer comparisons from nationally administered surveys, can contribute greatly to building a culture of evidence. Exercise 3.2—Fundamental Steps in Establishing a Culture of Evidence is helpful for student affairs leaders working to develop a culture of evidence on their campuses.

Importance of a Culture of Evidence in Student Affairs

SSAOs should consider what it means to have a culture of evidence in their division. The activities in this module are designed to help SSAOs examine this question. A culture of evidence demonstrates that the student affairs professionals have a vested interest in knowing how their programs and services are affecting students and other stakeholders, and that they use assessment results to improve programs and services.

Conditions Needed to Foster a Culture of Evidence

Suskie (2009) cited four keys to fostering a culture of evidence:

- ✪ Value campus culture and history.
- ✪ Respect and empower people.
- ✪ Value innovation and risk taking.
- ✪ Value assessment efforts.

Although these points are made in the context of a campuswide culture of evidence and assessment in academic programs, they are equally applicable to a culture of evidence in student affairs.

Seagraves and Dean (2010) examined the conditions that support a culture of assessment in divisions of student affairs at small colleges and universities (enrollment less than 5,000). Although their findings have not been generalized to other types of institutions, their conclusions are consistent with the widely accepted conditions necessary for developing and sustaining a culture of evidence. The conditions include the following:

- ✪ Support of the SSAO.
- ✪ Informal expectation that assessment activities will take place.
- ✪ Belief that assessment efforts lead to improvement in programs and services.
- ✪ Collegial working environment.

A culture of evidence will have different characteristics on different campuses, but many similarities will exist among institutions that are building and maintaining these efforts, including leadership, staff involvement, and use of results. The support and leadership of the SSAO paves the way for the culture of evidence to grow and develop in the division. However, developing a culture of evidence is a two-way street that runs not only from the top down but also from the bottom up, with support from mid- and early-career professionals. Staff members should have a shared understanding of and commitment to good assessment practices, and should be empowered and rewarded in their assessment and institutional effectiveness efforts. Improvements in programs and services should be evident and based on credible data.

Changing the Culture

Developing and sustaining a culture of evidence will likely require significant changes in your approach and that of your staff members as far as the collection and use of data to inform decision making. Managing change is one of the most difficult things a leader does. If you are not already familiar with the theories of change and best practices in leading change, consider familiarizing yourself with the models and stages of change and the leadership skills needed to navigate changes. Opportunities and challenges are present whenever change is considered. Exercise 3.5—Navigating Barriers and Opportunities is designed to help SSAOs identify the challenges and opportunities inherent in developing a culture of evidence on campus. Table 3.1 lists some common barriers and opportunities.

Table 3.1

Culture of Evidence: Barriers and Opportunities

Barriers	Opportunities
Campus culture	Campus culture
Lack of leadership support to provide direction and resources	Leaders who support assessment with time, infrastructure, and resources
Lack of assessment expertise and training	Professional development
Resistance to change	Leaders who can manage change
Disconnect between units and purposes of assessment	Staff who value assessment and can use results
Lack of reward for assessment efforts	Honors and rewards for assessment activities
Unrealistic expectations for assessment activities	Opportunities to build on past and current successes
Belief that assessment is for accountability, not improvement	Institution takes a proactive approach to gathering and using data
Budget and resource constraints	Assessment is taking place elsewhere on campus; collaboration is possible

Strategies for Creating a Culture of Evidence in Student Affairs

Develop a divisionwide vision for assessment, including mission, goals, and plans for activities. The vision for assessment is distinct from but complementary to the division's vision and mission statements. Having a plan for assessment activities is important, because there is always a temptation to focus on hot-button issues or the "problem du jour." Although it is often necessary to evaluate and act on current issues, a well-designed assessment plan will provide evidence in a systematic rather than a reactionary manner. A clear plan for assessment activities will set the course and direct the work of those responsible for the assessment. The vision for assessment can be developed by an assessment unit, a committee, or the SSAO. In determining the priorities for assessment, keep in mind the words often attributed to Albert Einstein: "Not everything that counts can be counted, and not everything that can be counted counts."

Work within the existing structures of the institution. To develop and sustain a culture of evidence, SSAOs should work within the existing campus climate and structure rather than going it alone—or worse, going against these structures. For example, student affairs should be represented on campuswide or universitywide assessment or planning committees. The Division of Student Affairs at Tulane University actively participates in the University Committee on Assessment. Leveraging existing structures within the division also helps—many campuses use divisionwide assessment committees to develop, execute, and integrate assessment activities.

Many institutions use a proprietary software system or locally developed reporting tool to support institutional effectiveness and accreditation efforts. If your institution has an established mechanism for reporting assessment activities, the division of student affairs should be included in that process.

Establish relationships with staff and faculty who promote a culture of evidence. Establish relationships with other campus professionals who are interested or engaged in assessment work. The SSAO should support such partnerships and encourage student affairs staff to collaborate with others engaging in similar work, including staff in the division of student affairs, the office of institutional research, or academic assessment; faculty with research interests or skills in related areas; and other stakeholders. Without these relationships and SSAO support for them, developing

QUICK TIP

The University of Alabama Division of Student Affairs has the following vision and mission for the Office of Student Affairs Assessment and Planning:

✿ Vision: To be an exemplary office of student affairs assessment that actively promotes assessment activities and contributes to the scholarship of assessment.

✿ Mission: The Office of Student Affairs Assessment and Planning serves the Division of Student Affairs and the University of Alabama by providing information, resources, expertise, and leadership to advance student learning and program effectiveness. (H. Hallmann, personal communication, May 25, 2012)

and sustaining a culture of evidence will be nearly impossible. In some cases, the SSAO may need to initiate dialogue about the culture of evidence with these potential campus partners.

Disseminate assessment-related information across the division. Communicating assessment activities and results to all division staff is critical to developing a culture of evidence. It is important for the SSAO and division leaders to receive and review assessment results, either as a full report or an executive summary. Results should also be shared with campus stakeholders who are engaging in assessment activities or who may benefit from the findings. Such dissemination provides an opportunity for staff to demonstrate their good work, fosters ideas among staff members, encourages collaboration, highlights best practices, acknowledges those who engage in such efforts, and can lead to scholarly presentations and publications. Assessment information can be distributed through websites, electronic newsletters, press releases, annual reports, and campus presentations or mini-conferences. The list of dissemination best practices that follows is only a small sample of the myriad resources readily available online.

Websites:

✿ University of North Carolina at Greensboro (http://sa.uncg.edu/assessment)

✿ John Carroll University (http://sites.jcu.edu/vpsa-assessment/pages/about)

✿ The Ohio State University (http://slra.osu.edu)

Newsletters:

⚙ University of Georgia (http://studentaffairs.uga.edu/assess/pulse/index.htm)

⚙ University of Oregon (http://newsletter.uoregon.edu)

Annual reports:

⚙ The University of Alabama (http://issuu.com/uastudentaffairs/docs/uastudentaffairshighlights/1)

⚙ California State University, Fullerton (http://www.fullerton.edu/sa/assessment/publications.aspx)

Presentations/mini-conferences:

⚙ Emory University (https://blogs.emory.edu/assessconference)

⚙ University of North Texas (http://studentaffairs.unt.edu/student-portrait-symposium)

⚙ Stanford University (http://www.stanford.edu/dept/pres-provost/cgi-bin/irds/wordpress/2010/07/student-affairs-assessment-poster-fair)

⚙ Duke University (http://studentaffairs.duke.edu/ra/assessment/2nd-annual-assessment-and-evaluation-poster-fair)

An assessment web page can provide a repository for division assessment results. This page can be included in the student affairs website as well as the institutional website dedicated to assessment, if one exists. In cases in which complete results cannot be published online, include an executive summary. Most divisions distribute an annual report to share information and to meet broader campus institutional effectiveness and accreditation requirements. If your division is not already developing and distributing an annual report, give serious consideration to doing so.

Engage in assessment-related professional development. Experts emphasize the importance of engaging faculty in assessment to improve assessment practices and develop a culture of evidence (e.g., Angelo, 2002; Banta 2002). This is true for student affairs staff as well. A culture of evidence is developed through ownership of the process, and student affairs professionals should learn the necessary skills. An SSAO who supports opportunities for professional development demonstrates the importance of a culture of evidence and generates buy-in from the staff.

Opportunities for professional development should not be overlooked, even in a time of constrained and disappearing resources. Professional development activities related to assessment can be offered at little or no cost and

QUICK TIP

Division assessment committees can provide leadership for assessment activities and professional development opportunities for staff, and can communicate results across the division.

still have a strong impact on staff members. For example, brown bag lunches or morning coffee groups bring professionals together to discuss assessment and institutional effectiveness practices. Although it can be difficult for staff to dedicate the time to meet, carefully designing such an activity can ensure that it is manageable. One option is to conduct these meetings as four- or six-week sessions at different times during the year. Not every staff member will be able to attend every session, but varying the topics and time periods can allow for greater overall participation. Organizing and implementing a common book experience is an excellent way to engage staff in the study of assessment and institutional effectiveness, and may serve as an opportunity for a new professional to facilitate or lead. Staff can participate in self-directed opportunities using as a guide the *Professional Competency Areas for Student Affairs Practitioners* (ACPA & NASPA, 2010), the Assessment Education Framework (NASPA

QUICK TIP

The following institutions are among those that have units or staff dedicated to student affairs assessment:

- Texas A&M University

- The University of Memphis

- University of North Carolina at Charlotte

- University of Georgia

Assessment, Evaluation, and Research Knowledge Community, 2009), or the ASK Standards (ACPA, 2007).

Building a library of assessment-related texts is a low-cost way to promote professional development. These books can be available for student affairs staff to borrow. Another low-cost strategy is to conduct unit-specific workshops on general or specific assessment topics to develop the skills and abilities of staff members. These workshops can be facilitated by members of the division who have the necessary skills and experience, or by campus partners such as faculty or institutional research professionals. Colleagues from other institutions might also facilitate these workshops. Although there may be some costs associated with bringing in an external speaker, the return on the investment might be very high for the staff.

Of course, there are myriad professional development opportunities through conferences and professional associations; the Resources section later in this module lists many of them. However, the most important factor is that SSAOs make professional development activities relevant and applicable.

Identify and involve assessment champions. Even in a division of student affairs with a strong culture of evidence, some staff members will participate in assessment efforts more actively than others. One strategy to develop and sustain a culture of evidence is to identify and involve staff members who are willing and able to lead this effort. This strategy has the added benefit of providing opportunities to share the assessment workload across the division.

Some institutions have a staff member or unit dedicated to student affairs assessment, research, and planning activities. Although these units are usually found on larger campuses, institutions of any size can choose an assessment champion in the division. The person charged with leading student affairs assessment can identify and coordinate assessment efforts across the division.

Identifying and involving assessment champions can contribute to developing a culture of evidence. First, SSAOs should define the expectations for these champions and determine their responsibilities, both formal and informal. Responsibilities might include facilitating professional development opportunities, holding periodic meetings, executing assessment efforts, and communicating with the division leadership team. SSAOs should ensure that staff members who are interested in becoming assessment champions possess the necessary skills and abilities to execute their responsibilities. If they do not possess the requisite skills, professional development and training can be provided.

Bringing together interested staff members can enable them to use the skills and knowledge they have gained and to share techniques and expertise with one another. In particular, bringing together staff from different units or departments in the division can help break down any silos that might exist in the division. Cross-functional committees and working groups are well positioned to examine divisionwide issues such as retention, and intradivision collaborations can create opportunities to combine survey efforts and reduce survey fatigue.

Eliminate assessment-related anxiety. SSAOs are uniquely positioned to help minimize staff anxiety related to assessment and a culture of evidence. Some staff members have concerns about gathering and using data in their decision-making processes, and in many cases those concerns are valid. Assessment results should be used to improve the division's programs and services, and the budgeting process should be linked to the planning and assessment processes. However, for new and seasoned professionals alike, the thought that a program or initiative might be eliminated because of unfavorable assessment results can turn a culture of evidence into a culture of fear. Assessment and personnel review activities should be conducted separately, and that separation should be clearly communicated across the division. Wherever possible, simplify the process. A strong culture of evidence is developed and sustained by using data and embracing a philosophy of informing decision making with the right information. Burdensome reporting obligations and cumbersome assessment plans are not necessary.

SSAOs can allay the fears of many staff members through frequent and consistent communication and by demonstrating their leadership and support for assessment. If you are in the early phases of developing a culture of evidence, start small, set clear expectations, be flexible, and be patient. It takes time for a culture to develop. Along the way, celebrate successes and reward assessment efforts.

READINESS TO DEVELOP A CULTURE OF EVIDENCE

As an SSAO you may understand the importance of fostering a culture of evidence but be unsure how to begin the process. Conducting a readiness review is an excellent first step. Exercise 3.4—What Does It Mean to Have a Culture of Evidence? and Exercise 3.6—Culture of Evidence Readiness Review are helpful for starting the process and will allow you to ascertain staff members' receptivity to a culture of evidence and willingness to change, as well as the level of assessment activity currently in place.

SSAOs are uniquely positioned to influence the culture of evidence on their campuses. They can set an example for their own staff through their support for assessment and, as campus leaders, they can contribute to the broader culture of evidence. Student affairs can be a valuable partner in this culture by gathering and sharing data that can be used by faculty and administrators.

Issac M. Carter, dean of students at St. Thomas University in Florida, and former student affairs program leader at both DePaul University in Illinois, and Humboldt State University in California, worked with his team of leaders in student affairs to develop a strategic plan and, ultimately, a culture of evidence in the department. Carter asked each unit leader to use the CAS SAGs as a tool to reshape the unit mission, job descriptions, and unit-level action plans. Staff members were assigned to working pairs across units to conduct program reviews and action plans. The team approach created constructive, divergent thinking; new opportunities for collaboration; and a support system for assessment within a culture of evidence. Beyond looking at their own programs, unit leaders focused on student development as a result of student affairs program participation. To examine programs and procedures, the teams used CAS standards (2009) and the *Professional Competency Areas for Student Affairs Practitioners* (ACPA & NASPA, 2010) as frameworks; to review student learning outcomes, the team used the learning and development outcome domains in the CAS standards. Having led the student affairs team through a thorough self-assessment process and a new operating philosophy that accentuates data-driven decision making, Carter offers the following pointers for fostering a culture of evidence:

1. Student affairs staff must positively reframe planning and assessment into a commonplace, intentional, professional practice rather than an additional chore necessary only for accreditation compliance or funding.

2. Student affairs staff must be able to link planning and assessment at both the macro levels of accreditation, strategic planning, and institutional budget allocation and the micro levels of program implementation and student learning outcomes.

3. SSAOs must use the terminology of planning and assessment in every aspect of the division, including job descriptions, staff meetings, program proposals, incentives, and resource development.

4. Each student affairs staff member must be developed as a scholar-practitioner in his or her unit and as part of the overall higher education profession. Unit programs must be steeped in research and best practices to develop an evidence-based culture.

5. Student affairs staff must develop the planning and assessment tools necessary to evaluate the achievement of desired outcomes as part of the strategic planning processes. It is important to have the right tools to perform the job.

6. Student affairs staff must have regular work time scheduled for planning and assessment.

7. Student affairs professionals must share the results of their planning and assessment within the division and with the wider university community.

8. SSAOs must make a culture of evidence a planning priority in their overall leadership and management objectives.

9. SSAOs need to develop strong relationships with institutional research, assessment, and planning offices.

10. Student affairs staff must model a culture of evidence when they are working with other areas of the campus community.

11. Student affairs staff must do their homework. Each member of the staff must work individually to deepen his or her knowledge of planning and assessment. (I. Carter, personal communication, April 17, 2012)

Zebulun R. Davenport, vice chancellor for student life at Indiana University–Purdue University Indianapolis (IUPUI) and former vice president for student affairs at Northern Kentucky University (NKU), has fostered cultures of evidence successfully throughout his career. Whether a culture of evidence in student affairs is emerging or established, Davenport cites leadership, systematic assessment efforts, and use of results as key factors for success.

A culture of evidence can only be developed with the commitment of SSAOs. Davenport emphasizes the importance of a culture of evidence with his staff and makes sure they understand the benefits that accrue to the division when a culture of evidence is prevalent. He describes the importance of leadership in this process: "Without the support of the divisional leaders, there will be no culture of evidence. It is that simple." Davenport says that having a staff member dedicated to assessment "emphasizes the importance of this work to the profession." At NKU, Davenport created two positions: senior analyst for planning and budgeting, and senior analyst for assessment and evaluation. He says this decision "illustrated the dedication and importance of assessment to our work." At IUPUI, Davenport has been "intentional about positioning and empowering the director of planning and assessment in such a way that his role has authority and prominence, and is essential to our work."

To be effective, assessment efforts should be executed in a systematic manner according to an established plan. Davenport says that assessment activities might already be taking place across the division, but staff needed help articulating their efforts more formally. He makes a point of celebrating their accomplishments, promoting a common language of assessment, and creating mechanisms to assess the impact of learning. He is also asking staff to link programs to learning outcomes that promote student success. In particular, Davenport intends to link "resources to projects and initiatives that use evidence to show impact and illustrate effective partnerships related to certain existing academic initiatives, such as the IUPUI Principles of Undergraduate Learning (PULs), and other constructs that address learning not included in the PULs." This effort also demonstrates how the culture of evidence in student life supports the institution.

Using results to inform decision making is a hallmark of Davenport's efforts. He not only uses results to support student learning outcomes and program goals but also uses data to inform the strategic planning process. He conducted a gap analysis to determine strengths, weaknesses, opportunities, and challenges, and used focus group and interview results to create a situational analysis. Davenport describes his work this way: "Based on the findings of the gap analysis and situational analysis, members of the leadership team and I prioritized the most urgent needs of the division and constructed a plan to fill the gaps. As a result of this work, we reorganized the division to maximize the strengths of professionals and functions of our departments to address student needs. We also used this data to create a new department to resolve problems expressed by the constituents included in the gap analysis." To foster a culture of evidence, Davenport says, "Assessment is not an unnecessary second step, it is a crucial first step." He reminds us to create "learning constructs that match the skills and competencies that the literature identifies as being critical to student success" (Z. Davenport, personal communication, May 25, 2012).

Developing a leadership team to establish and maintain a culture of evidence may be challenging, but the effort will prove to be rewarding in terms of staff effectiveness, program quality, and student growth. Using data to evaluate the degree to which students attain important skills and knowledge that student affairs staff have identified as critical to personal, academic, and career success allows for the improvement of staff efforts and better student outcomes. Further, the ability to demonstrate the integral value of student support services vis-à-vis student learning establishes the vital role of student affairs in the full development of students.

APPLY THE CONCEPTS

Exercise 3.1—*Reflection Questions for Developing Your Mission and Vision*

Directions: Answer the following questions individually and as a team to develop your mission and vision.

Student Affairs Mission Statement
Who are we?
What do we do?
What is our purpose?
Where is the alignment between the institution's mission and core values and the student affairs mission?

Student Affairs Vision Statement
With the right effort and the right resources, what will our student affairs division look like in 5 or 10 years?
What will our students know?
How will they be different because of our programs and services?

APPLY THE CONCEPTS

Exercise 3.2—*Fundamental Steps in Establishing a Culture of Evidence*

Directions: Answer the following questions that anchor the steps in establishing a culture of evidence. Use various configurations of teams to discuss the questions and develop responses.

Step	Reflection
Review your mission.	Who are we?
Articulate your vision.	Who do we want to be?
Complete an environmental scan and review professional standards.	What should we know?
Create an action plan.	Why should we care? What is the endpoint? How do we get there? Are we there yet?

APPLY THE CONCEPTS

Exercise 3.3—*What Do You Mean By...?*

This activity is designed as a catalyst for discussing and establishing common terminology.

PART 1

Directions: Listed below are a number of terms related to a culture of evidence. Each person should consider the item and indicate with a checkmark his or her familiarity with the term.

	I have never heard this term before.	I recognize this term, but I do not know what it means.	I know this term, and I have a vague understanding of what it means.	I understand this term and could explain its meaning to someone else.
Culture of evidence				
Anecdotal culture				
Assessment				
Institutional effectiveness				
Learning outcome				
Goals				
Objectives				
Indirect measure				
Direct measure				
Accountability				

Discussion: After everyone has completed the table above, discuss the responses. Why are some terms more familiar than others? What are the gaps in knowledge of these concepts?

PART 2

Directions: Individually or as a group, provide a brief definition and an example for each term.

	Definition	Example
Culture of evidence		
Anecdotal culture		
Assessment		
Institutional effectiveness		
Learning outcome		
Goals		
Objectives		
Indirect measure		
Direct measure		
Accountability		

Discussion: If this exercise is completed individually, participants are encouraged to discuss their definitions and examples as a group. Is there a common understanding of the terms? If not, what are the differences? Which terms are unclear?

APPLY THE CONCEPTS

Exercise 3.4—*What Does It Mean to Have a Culture of Evidence?*

Directions: Using a think-pair-share strategy, each person should complete the following worksheet independently, then the group should share responses.

At Your Institution	
Describe your institutional assessment activities.	**Describe the assessment activities in the division of student affairs.**
Defining Your Culture of Evidence	
Describe your division's current culture of evidence.	**Provide your vision of a culture of evidence.**
Closing the Gap	
What are the gaps between the current culture of evidence and the desired culture of evidence?	**State possible solutions to close the gaps between the current and desired cultures of evidence.**

Discussion: In what ways would the division of student affairs be transformed by a culture of evidence? How would a culture of evidence affect the vision, mission, and goals of the division?

APPLY THE CONCEPTS

Exercise 3.5—*Navigating Barriers and Opportunities*

Directions: Using a think-pair-share strategy, each person should answer the following questions independently, then the group should share responses.

What are the barriers to developing a culture of evidence in your division of student affairs?
Which of these barriers can you directly influence?
What opportunities exist on your campus or in your division that could enhance a culture of evidence in student affairs?
How can student affairs leverage available structures or opportunities to develop a culture of evidence?
Are there any opportunities to institutionalize current practices to foster a culture of evidence?

Discussion: How can you minimize the barriers that exist? How can you prevent new barriers from developing? How can you maximize the opportunities to enhance the culture of evidence? How can you promote additional opportunities in the future?

▶ APPLY THE CONCEPTS

Exercise 3.6—*Culture of Evidence Readiness Review*

Directions: Check all the statements that apply to your division of student affairs. Provide examples, where applicable, of how the statements are enacted in your division. This checklist is not designed to be a test; rather, it should be used to facilitate discussion and reflection on the current culture of evidence.

_____ Division has a vision and mission statement.

_____ SSAO is committed to building a culture of evidence.

_____ Staff members are committed to building a culture of evidence.

_____ Staff members are expected to use credible evidence to inform decisions.

_____ Division has a staff member or committee designated to lead assessment efforts.

_____ Division articulates divisionwide student learning outcomes/program goals.

_____ Departments within the division have outcomes for programs and services.

_____ Programs and services are linked directly to outcomes.

_____ Division has a practical and sustainable assessment plan.

_____ Assessment is conducted in a systematic manner.

_____ Data gathered and used are credible.

_____ Assessment results are communicated appropriately within the division.

_____ Assessment results are communicated appropriately to stakeholders.

_____ Changes and improvements are connected to evidence-based decisions.

_____ Division engages in institutionwide institutional effectiveness practices.

_____ Division uses the common language of assessment.

_____ Culture of evidence is valued by staff.

_____ Staff members use data in decision-making processes.

_____ Use of evidence-based decision making is included in staff responsibilities/job descriptions.

_____ Staff members have the necessary skills and knowledge to execute assessment.

_____ Assessment-related professional development opportunities are available for staff.

_____ Staff members are recognized for their assessment efforts.

_____ Division celebrates and rewards activities that promote a culture of evidence.

_____ Partnerships exist with other campus units to gather and use data.

_____ Division has a web presence dedicated to assessment efforts.

_____ Resources are available to conduct assessment activities.

_____ Best practices (CAS, etc.) are used.

_____ New programs and initiatives include assessment and evaluation.

RESOURCES

American College Personnel Association. (n.d.). Commission for Assessment and Evaluation. Retrieved from http://www.myacpa.org/comm/assessment

American College Personnel Association (ACPA) & National Association of Student Personnel Administrators (NASPA), Joint Task Force on Professional Competencies and Standards. (2010). *Professional competency areas for student affairs practitioners*. Retrieved from http://www.naspa.org/programs/prodev/Professional_Competencies.pdf

Association of American Colleges and Universities. (n.d.). *Assessment*. Retrieved from http://www.aacu.org/resources/assessment/index.cfm

Association for Institutional Research. (n.d.). *IR links–quality–assessment*. Retrieved from http://www.airweb.org/Resources/Links/Pages/LinksQualityAssessment.aspx

Beede, M., & Burnett, D. J. (Eds.). (1999). *Planning for student services: Best practices for the 21ˢᵗ century*. Ann Arbor, MI: Society for College and University Planning.

Bowling Green State University. (n.d.). Student affairs history project. Retrieved from http://www.bgsu.edu/colleges/library/cac/sahp/index.htm

Burnett, D. J, & Oblinger, D. G. (Eds.). (2002). *Innovation in student services: Planning for models blending high touch/high tech*. Ann Arbor, MI: Society for College and University Planning.

Council for the Advancement of Standards in Higher Education (CAS). (2006). *CAS characteristics of individual excellence for professional practice in higher education*. Retrieved from http://www.cas.edu/wp-content/uploads/2011/03/CASIndividualExcellence.pdf

Council for the Advancement of Standards in Higher Education (CAS). (2006). *CAS statement of shared ethical principles*. Retrieved from http://www.cas.edu/wp-content/uploads/2010/08/CASethicsstatement.pdf

Council for the Advancement of Standards in Higher Education (CAS). (2006). *Frameworks for assessing learning and development outcomes*. Washington, DC: Author.

Council for the Advancement of Standards in Higher Education (CAS). (2008). *Council for the advancement of standards learning and developmental outcomes*. Retrieved from http://www.cas.edu/wp-content/uploads/2010/12/Learning-and-Developmental-Outcomes-2009.pdf

Council for the Advancement of Standards in Higher Education (CAS). (2012). *CAS professional standards for higher education*. Washington, DC: Author.

Council for the Advancement of Standards in Higher Education (CAS). (2012). *CAS self-assessment guides*. Washington, DC: Author.

Educational Testing Service. (n.d.). *Culture of evidence overview*. Retrieved from http://www.ets.org/culture_evidence

Higher Education Resource Hub. (n.d.). *Assessment in higher education*. Retrieved from http://www.higher-ed.org/resources/Assessment.htm

Keeling, R. P. (Ed.). (2004). *Learning reconsidered: A campus-wide focus on the student experience.* Washington, DC: American College Personnel Association and National Association of Student Personnel Administrators.

Keeling, R. P. (Ed.). (2006). *Learning reconsidered 2: A practical guide to implementing a campus-wide focus on the student learning experience.* Washington, DC: American College Personnel Association, Association of College and University Housing Officers–International, Association of College Unions International, National Academic Advising Association, National Association for Campus Activities, National Association of Student Personnel Administrators, and National Intramural-Recreational Sports Association.

Oburn, M. (2005). Building a culture of evidence in student affairs. In S. R. Helfgot & M. M. Culp (Eds.), *Community college student affairs: What really matters* (New directions for community colleges, no. 131, pp. 19–32). San Francisco, CA: Jossey-Bass.

National Association of Student Personnel Administrators. (n.d.). Assessment, evaluation, and research knowledge community. Retrieved from http://www.naspa.org/kc/saaer/default.cfm

National Association of Student Personnel Administrators. (n.d.). NASPA assessment and persistence conference. Retrieved from http://naspa.org/programs/apc/default.cfm

National Institute for Learning Outcomes Assessment. (n.d.). Resources. Retrieved from http://www.learningoutcomeassessment.org/Resources.htm

Society for College and University Planning. (2001–2005). *Assessment and quality* [SCUP Portfolio]. Ann Arbor, MI: Author.

Society for College and University Planning. (2008–2009). *Make way for millennials: How students are shaping learning in higher education* [SCUP Portfolio]. Ann Arbor, MI: Author.

Society for College and University Planning. (n.d.). Retrieved from http://www.scup.org/page/index

The TLT Group. (2007). Dealing with resistance to your study. Retrieved from http://www.tltgroup.org/Flashlight/Handbook/Resistance.htm

References

American College Personnel Association (ACPA). (2007). *ASK standards.* Washington, DC: Author.

American College Personnel Association (ACPA) & National Association of Student Personnel Administrators (NASPA), Joint Task Force on Professional Competencies and Standards. (2010). *Professional competency areas for student affairs practitioners.* Retrieved from http://www.naspa.org/programs/prodev/Professional_Competencies.pdf

Angelo, T. A. (1999). Doing assessment as if learning matters most. *AAHE Bulletin, 51*(9), 3–6.

Angelo, T. A. (2002). Engaging and supporting faculty in the scholarship of assessment. In T. W. Banta (Ed.), *Building a scholarship of assessment* (pp. 185–200). San Francisco, CA: Jossey-Bass.

Banta, T. W. (Ed.). (2002). *Building a scholarship of assessment.* San Francisco, CA: Jossey-Bass.

Banta, T. W. (Ed.). (2004). *Hallmarks of effective outcomes assessment.* San Francisco, CA: Jossey-Bass.

Boone, L. E., & Kurtz, D. L. (1995). *Contemporary marketing.* Hinsdale, IL: Dryden Press.

Collins, J. (2000, June). Aligning action and values. *Forum.* Retrieved from http://www.jimcollins.com/article_topics/articles/aligning-action.html.

Council for the Advancement of Standards in Higher Education (CAS). (2008). *Council for the advancement of standards learning and developmental outcomes.* Retrieved from http://www.cas.edu/wp-content/uploads/2010/12/Learning-and-Developmental-Outcomes-2009.pdf

Council for the Advancement of Standards in Higher Education (CAS). (2009). *CAS professional standards for higher education.* Washington, DC: Author.

Council for the Advancement of Standards in Higher Education (CAS). (2012). *CAS professional standards for higher education.* Washington, DC: Author.

Dooris, M. J. (2003). Two decades of strategic planning. *Planning for Higher Education, 31*(2), 26–32.

Erwin, T. D. (1991). *Assessing student learning and development: A guide to the principles, goals, and methods of determining college outcomes.* San Francisco, CA: Jossey-Bass.

Head, R. B. (2011). The evolution of institutional effectiveness in the community college. In R. B. Head (Ed.), *Institutional Effectiveness* (New directions for community colleges, no. 153, pp. 5–11). San Francisco, CA: Jossey-Bass.

Keeling, R. P. (Ed.). (2004). *Learning reconsidered: A campus-wide focus on the student experience.* Washington, DC: American College Personnel Association and National Association of Student Personnel Administrators.

Keeling, R. P. (Ed.). (2006). *Learning reconsidered 2: A practical guide to implementing a campus-wide focus on the student learning experience.* Washington, DC: American College Personnel Association, Association of College and University Housing Officers–International, Association of College Unions International, National Academic Advising Association, National Association for Campus Activities, National Association of Student Personnel Administrators, and National Intramural-Recreational Sports Association.

NASPA Assessment, Evaluation, and Research Knowledge Community. (2009). *Assessment education framework*. Retrieved from http://www.naspa.org/kc/saaer/FrameworkBrochure-Dec09.pdf

Seagraves, B., & Dean, L. A. (2010). Conditions supporting a culture of evidence in student affairs divisions at small colleges and universities. *Journal of Student Affairs Research and Practice, 47*(3), 307–324.

Suskie, L. (2009). *Assessing student learning: A common sense guide* (2nd ed.). San Francisco, CA: Jossey-Bass.

TLT Group. (n.d.). *Strengthening an institution's culture of evidence*. Retrieved May 26, 2012, from http://www.tltgroup.org/flashlight/Handbook/culture-evidence.htm

MODULE 4

Using Outcomes and Rubrics in Student Affairs

Tisa A. Mason and Shana Warkentine Meyer

I**N THE PAST 20 YEARS,** student affairs divisions have placed a higher priority on assessment. However, some professionals have focused primarily on student learning outcomes (SLOs) as a one-dimensional approach in their culture of evidence initiatives. Is this approach to assessment adequate, or do professionals risk sending an incomplete message about the importance of student affairs to the rest of the institution when relying on one type of data?

The feedback from practitioners in the field is mixed. For some, the importance of learning outcomes is key. Fernando Padro, a Faculty Fellow in NASPA–Student Affairs Administrators in Higher Education and chair-elect of the Education Division of the American Society for Quality, says:

> The era of the learner outcome is here to stay for the foreseeable future. As someone who studies trends in quality assurance processes in the USA and abroad, [I can say that] learner outcomes are now so universally used that going to something else may challenge the profession's credibility or expansion of use in other national systems. (personal communication, April 23, 2012)

While respecting the critical and valuable nature of assessment, other professionals believe there may be risk in focusing too much on learning outcomes. Zauyah Waite, vice president for student affairs and dean of students at Chatham University in Pennsylvania, says:

The reality is that we live in an academic world and, as a result, assessment is and always will be a critical part of our culture and environment. However, I strongly caution that if we in student affairs tend to focus solely on learning outcomes, we risk losing the incidental learning moments that come with the unstructured framework of what students and professional do so frequently. (personal communication, May 10, 2012)

Timothy R. Ecklund, associate vice president for campus life at Buffalo State College in New York, shares his thoughts on senior student affairs officers' focus on student learning outcomes:

The pressures to demonstrate to students, accrediting agencies, and budget officers the efficacy of what we do have never been so great. This raises questions: Will SLOs define student affairs in the future or should SLOs just be another tool to use in addressing our complex challenges in this new culture of evidence? In the new culture of evidence, are SLOs key to the survival of student affairs? Can we really demonstrate how students learn and develop using SLOs? What do we base our SLOs on?

It is my fear that we will run headstrong into the creation and use of SLOs without really understanding their purpose, place, and effective use. As such, we risk misinterpreting the intent of SLOs. SLOs are intended to create a large overarching feedback loop to map change, not to be used as simple classroom objectives. SLOs have an important place in our work but are only a piece of a much larger picture of student learning." (personal communication, May 29, 2012).

 IN THE SPOTLIGHT

"Lee Upcraft and I published a series of books and papers in the 1990s and early 2000s that were designed to add a practical dimension to assessment and evaluation in student affairs. At the many workshops and presentations that we did, we often asked the question, 'How many of you got into student affairs practice because you wanted to do assessment work?' Rarely did any of the participants raise their hands. We found that participants, in many cases, needed to be convinced that engaging in assessment was necessary. We also found that while they may have studied assessment and evaluation techniques in graduate school, these courses were among their least favorite and rarely had they incorporated assessment into their practice as student affairs educators. We worked to change their minds and encourage them to begin the process of determining the effectiveness of their work." —*John H. Schuh, distinguished professor of educational leadership and policy studies emeritus, Iowa State University (personal communication, May 24, 2012)*

Lori Reesor, vice president for student affairs at the University of North Dakota, agrees:

> It's more complicated than SLOs. It is challenging to effectively assess for academic decision makers the value of student involvement and student life components. For example, have we clearly demonstrated to our campuses that residence halls are more than places to live, socialize, and study? Can we document the outside-the-classroom learning that occurs by living in a residence hall? Everything we do must support the academic mission and be connected to that mission. And sometimes we [student affairs] operate more in isolation and need a stronger connection to the academic divisions. (personal communication, April 25, 2012)

Robert D. Reason, associate professor of student affairs and higher education at Iowa State University, argues that student affairs professionals do a disservice by narrowly defining student learning outcomes to exclude student developmental outcomes. He says:

> It seems a very appropriate time to engage in a broad conversation about what constitutes 'learning' and what constitutes "development," and how these concepts relate to one another. Student affairs professionals have a much less well defined/articulated understanding of development (our supposed focus) than do those folks who are concerned about student learning. I believe we could do ourselves a service by (1) coming to a shared understanding of development and its relationship to learning and (2) determining how we integrate this shared understanding into the broader discourse on learning. Learning and development are inextricably interrelated. There is not one without the other, and to pit them against each other hurts us and, more importantly, our students. (personal communication, April 25, 2012)

IN THE SPOTLIGHT

"When we were working on what became *Learning Reconsidered* (Keeling, 2004), we wanted to articulate that academic learning and personal development were not opposite sides of a coin but on the same side and dynamically intertwined. We hoped the word learning could be 'reconsidered' to mean both academic learning and personal development . . . and feared that the word would come to mean only academic learning, as I think has happened for those who do not know the philosophy behind *Learning Reconsidered*. I fully support and consistently try to use the language of learning and personal development, or we present an incomplete understanding of the complexity we are seeking to promote." —*Susan R. Komives, professor emeritus of college student personnel, University of Maryland, College Park; president, Council for the Advancement of Standards in Higher Education; co-primary investigator, Multi-Institutional Study of Leadership; author,* Learning Reconsidered *(personal communication, April 25, 2012)*

Marilee Bresciani, professor of administration, rehabilitation, and postsecondary education at San Diego State University, concurs:

> If we toss out our commitment to intentionally designing and evaluating all systems as they relate to the facilitation of holistic student learning and development, then it is my humble opinion that we have lost the very essence of why our profession was created in the first place. I don't believe we are able to assess everything we do. But I do believe we can become more committed to articulating how the intention (i.e., outcomes) of everything we do exists to facilitate or support whole-person education and development. I believe we should allow holistic or integrated student learning and development to drive the way in which we organize ourselves and deliver our services and curriculum. If we can't articulate why what we do advances the wholeness of the human experience in education, then what exactly is our purpose and how will assessment inform that conversation? (personal communication, May 20, 2012)

This module focuses on the importance of creating a culture of evidence that includes learning outcomes, developmental outcomes, program outcomes, and a variety of assessment strategies, including rubrics. Definitions and examples for each are provided, with best practices from many institutions. The module concludes with an application exercise that may be used individually or departmentally, and resources for further information.

THE CULTURE OF EVIDENCE CONTINUUM

How do student affairs professionals exercise due diligence in relation to demonstrating the contributions of student affairs to the institution's missions and goals? As Table 4.1 illustrates, the options range from building a culture of good intentions to creating a culture of evidence. The goal, of course, is to create a true culture of evidence through a variety of assessment strategies, including learning, developmental, and program outcomes, as well as rubrics. After reviewing the information in this section, readers may access the PowerPoint presentation Using Outcomes for Assessment: A Checklist for Identifying and Articulating Measurable Outcomes (available at http://www.naspa. org/cultureofevidence/MOD4PP.pdf).

Learning Outcomes

Learning outcomes assess the intellectual or cognitive learning that you want to occur, not emotional or affective measurements. According to Witt (n.d.), a good learning outcome has eight components: (1) audience, (2) program/service, (3) learning expected, (4) specific qualifiers, (5) measurement (tools and process), (6) responsible parties (for measurement, follow-up, and reporting), (7) a timeframe, and (8) external standards. These components can be turned into a student learning outcome template, for example: (1) All (4) incoming students who complete the (2) New Student Orientation program (3) will be able to identify at least one (4) way in which they plan to get involved with student life outside the classroom. (7) During the final session of each orientation program, (6)

Table 4.1

Measuring a Culture of Evidence

	Culture of Good Intentions	Culture of Justification	Culture of Strategy	Culture of Evidence
Intentionality	People have a sense that they are doing good things.	People can describe what they are *doing* (i.e., operational or procedural specificity) .	People can describe what they are *accomplishing* (i.e., strategic pertinence, how what they are doing relates to mission and goals).	People know that they are doing the right things and can describe why they are doing them and what they are accomplishing.
Perspective	Incidental/opportunistic: Recognize that data are important, but do not make any particular efforts to collect them.	After the fact: Data are used retroactively as justification for predetermined positions or previous decisions.	Before the fact: Assessment is designed with an end in mind(e.g., identification of learning outcomes, how the data will be used).	Real time/continuous: Data are collected and regularly used to inform processes. Data help *close the loop* on improvement processes and educational outcomes.
Critical links	Opaque: Data, when collected, are not shared beyond assessors, so connections cannot be made.	Cloudy: Assessment is conducted from a defensive posture, especially related to questions of budgetary and operational efficiency.	Translucent: Assessment is understood and shared but only with allies or key partners. Scope is limited to midlevel managers.	Transparent: Outsiders can see and understand contributions to student and institutional success. Assessment is shared with all stakeholders.
Initiatives and directions	Determined by whim, interest, opportunity.	Administration initiates assessment and it is done only when asked for or required.	Directors own and initiate assessment. Data describe the current situation.	All stakeholders own assessment. Success is operationalized, concretely described, and evaluated on the basis of evidence.
Planning processes	Vague and individualized: Success is vague or interpretive and evaluated on the basis of "feel," intent, and effort. Collective or strategic planning does not exist.	Sporadic and limited to immediate question or application: Data are linked retroactively to strategic context, goals, and expectations, but the process is *not planning oriented*.	Organized, routinized, and localized: Data inform deliberate *cyclical or episodic strategic planning* exercises.	Ongoing, strategic, and clearly linked to past and future: Triangulation of findings through multiple/established assessments. Data are incorporated into *continuous strategic thinking*.

Note. Reprinted from *CSI Student Affairs: Creating a Culture of Evidence* [PowerPoint slides], by B. Spurlock and A. Feder, 2012, retrieved from http://convention.myacpa.org/archive/programs/Louisville12/index.html#csievidence. Reprinted with permission.

IN THE SPOTLIGHT

"Lee [Upcraft] and I defined assessment in 1996 as 'any effort to gather, analyze, and interpret evidence which describes institutional, divisional, or agency effectiveness.' We added, 'Effectiveness includes not only student learning outcomes, but assessing other important outcomes, such as cost-effectiveness, client satisfaction, meeting client needs, complying with professional standards, and comparisons with other institutions' (Schuh & Upcraft, 2001, p. 4)." —*John H. Schuh, distinguished professor of educational leadership and policy studies emeritus, Iowa State University (personal communication, May 24, 2012)*

orientation staff will (5) ask students to check areas of interest as part of the program evaluation (6) and each student will receive follow up from appropriate student affairs personnel. (8) This outcome is in compliance with First Year Information Grant stipulations.

One challenge in assessing learning is that students do not experience college in a way that makes outcome assessment simple. In addition, some learning outcomes may take months, years, or a lifetime to manifest. Assessing learning is more time-consuming and more difficult than other assessments, and indirect measures may not be accurate. Finally, open-ended survey questions do not provide quantitative data (Feder et al., 2011).

Bloom's Taxonomy (1956) is often used as a reference in writing student learning outcomes. The cognitive domain involves knowledge and the development of intellectual skills. As Table 4.1 demonstrates, the categories, listed from simplest to most complex, provide a list of verbs that can be used to write precise learning outcomes.

Figure 4.1

Bloom's Taxonomy — Cognitive

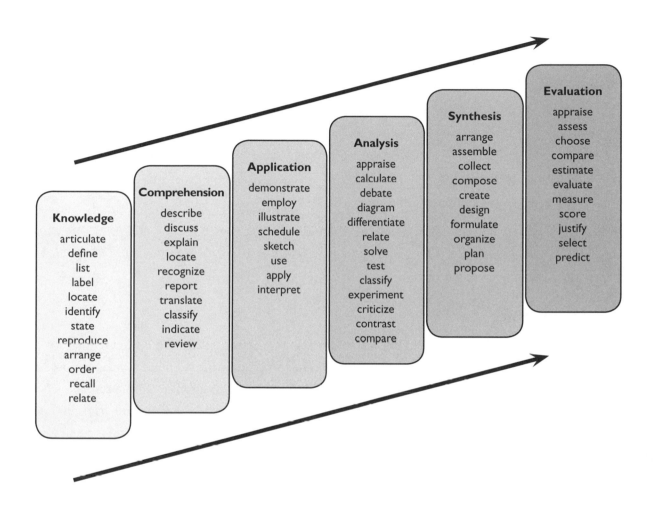

One test of a learning objective is Knirk and Gustafson's (1986) ABCD method. A well-written learning objective has four parts: A–audience, B–behavior, C–condition, and D–degree of measurement. Audience may include who is to perform the behavior, the person's level or rank, and when he or she is expected to perform the behavior. Behavior is an observable or measurable action. Condition is the situation under which the behavior is to be performed; for example, what resources will be available. Degree of measurement evaluates mastery of the behavior, which relates directly to the criteria component of a three-part objective. Commonly used criteria include accuracy (number and type of errors), speed, distance, and quantity (Knirk & Gustafson, 1986). An example of a direct learning outcome using the four components is: *After attending a sexual assault program, the learner (audience) will be given a worksheet of 50 multiple-choice questions (condition) and will select the correct answers (behavior) for at least 85% of the problems (degree of measurement).*

Developmental Outcomes

Developmental outcomes assess affective dimensions or attitudes directed toward a person (including oneself), object, place, or idea that predispose people to behave in certain ways (Bresciani, 2001). Developmental outcome statements describe the affective dimensions to be instilled or enhanced; assess affective dimensions or attitudes and values (not cognitive abilities); and consider growth in ethical, spiritual, emotional, and social responsibility dimensions (Denny, 2009). Examples of developmental outcomes include:

- ✿ Being sensitive to the values of others.
- ✿ Becoming aware of one's own talents and abilities.
- ✿ Developing an appreciation for lifelong learning.
- ✿ Practicing ethical behavior.
- ✿ Exhibiting personal discipline. (Denny, 2009)

An example of a developmental outcome is: *Students participating in the Tiger Service Clean and Green event will show evidence of increased civic responsibility as measured by increased civic responsibility correlation on the pretest/posttest.*

Program Outcomes

Program outcomes describe what you want your program to accomplish. They differ from learning outcomes in that they measure whether or not a specific program achieved what it was supposed to achieve when it was designed. Too often, program outcomes are measured in simple terms, such as "Was the task or activity completed?" This kind of measurement is rarely meaningful, as it does not provide information necessary for continuous improvement. A more useful approach is to assess the effectiveness of what you want to accomplish in your program.

For example, a program goal might be stated as: *The Academic Achievement Career Exploration Office will advise all undeclared students of all racial groups represented in the undeclared student population.* In this outcome, there is no stated intention of assessing learning, development, or quality of service. In addition, the outcome does not attempt to assess the level of satisfaction of all races with advising; it only attempts to assess whether undeclared students of all races were advised (Bresciani, 2001). Simply stated, a program outcome is the desired aggregate effect of a program, service, or intervention (Henning, 2010). Another sample program outcome is: *At least 80% of all students will lead a student organization during their college career.*

Rubrics

Campbell, Melenyzer, Nettles, and Wyman (2000) defined a rubric as multi-leveled or ranked criteria, tabled with a scale to measure and evaluate students' work. Rubrics provide *qualitative descriptions* of student learning and *quantitative results.* They can be used to assess observed practices, such as presentations, teamwork, trainings, role-plays, and performances. They can also be effectively used to analyze artifacts such as reflection papers, portfolios, journals, art pieces, and resumes (Feder et al., 2011).

Figure 4.2

The Components of a Rubric

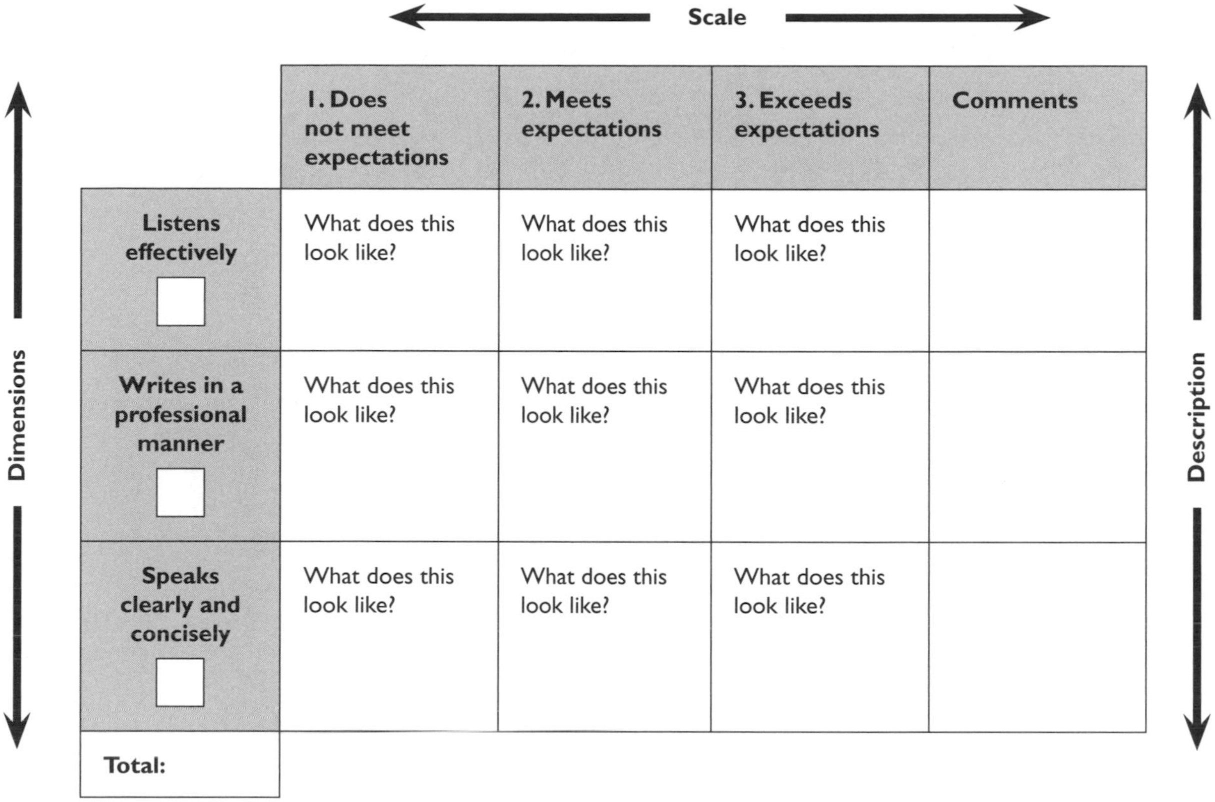

	1. Does not meet expectations	2. Meets expectations	3. Exceeds expectations	Comments
Listens effectively ☐	What does this look like?	What does this look like?	What does this look like?	
Writes in a professional manner ☐	What does this look like?	What does this look like?	What does this look like?	
Speaks clearly and concisely ☐	What does this look like?	What does this look like?	What does this look like?	
Total:				

Scale (horizontal axis). *Dimensions* (left vertical axis). *Description* (right vertical axis).

ASSESSMENT PLANS

A true culture of evidence begins with a comprehensive plan tied to the department or university mission. Gavin Henning (2012), founder and chair of Student Affairs Assessment Leaders, wrote that assessment is not an activity—it is a state of mind. He listed six steps one must follow to be a successful, strategic assessor:

1. **REFLECT.** The first step is to reflect on the issue or problem to be addressed—breaking it down into its elemental components to fully understand the complete scope of the issue.

2. **SET GOAL(S).** The second step is determining what you want to achieve in resolving the problem or issue, then developing the goals and outcomes that concretely conceptualize the end result. Think about "backwards" design; that is, decide what you want to achieve, then draw a road map that will get you to your destination. Depending on the issue, you may need to set short-, medium-, and long-term goals. For example, with regard to alcohol use on

campus, is the goal to decrease the number of hospitalizations per academic year, reduce the mean blood alcohol level of students taking an annual survey, or reduce the number of alcohol incidents in the residence halls during spring term? These are very different goals and require different routes to reach them.

3. **CONSIDER.** The third step is to consider the issues that will affect goal achievement. Consideration should include analyzing the institution's mission and culture, evaluating the literature and recent research to better understand the issue, and understanding the stakeholders and their perspectives. It is essential to realistically evaluate the resources available to address the issue or problem. Remember that resources are more than just money; they include fiscal, physical, human, and intellectual resources.

4. **STRATEGIZE.** This step focuses on identifying strategies and action steps to address the problem.

5. **MEASURE.** Measurement serves two purposes: It helps document outcomes and goal achievement, and it identifies areas for improvement. Improvement does not imply that goals were not achieved; rather, that there may be ways to achieve them more effectively or efficiently.

6. **REPORT and REFINE.** The final step is to share results with the appropriate constituent groups. If the goals were achieved, the recommendations for improvement should be implemented. Without this step, the assessment process is incomplete.

BEST PRACTICES

Developmental, learning, and program assessment have a place in all major areas in student affairs. As shown in the following examples, colleges and universities across the United States are employing a variety of learning outcomes, developmental outcomes, program outcomes, and other assessment strategies, including rubrics.

Academic Advising

At The University of Vermont, the division of Academic Support Programs tracks usage; conducts needs assessment of faculty, students, and volunteers in the Note Taking Program; tracks student grade point average and retention through outcomes assessment; provides satisfaction studies; measures its resource effectiveness; and sets benchmarking standards. To strategically plan for the future, the division uses CAS standards to review the program with an external panel (Assessment Continuum, 2010). The University of Wisconsin–Milwaukee's College of Engineering and Applied Science uses cognitive, skills, and affective student learning outcomes to measure the value of its academic advising (ACCESS to Success, 2011).

Admissions

The Office of Admission and Financial Aid at Pitzer College in California has created a goal for prospective students and their families to demonstrate learning outcomes. To achieve the eight established student learning outcomes, the office created eight means of communication, ranging from

IN THE SPOTLIGHT

Dan Bureau, director of student affairs learning and assessment at the University of Memphis in Tennessee, offers four strategies for writing learning outcomes:

○ **Use a framework.** The Council for the Advancement of Standards in Higher Education (CAS) lists six learning domains, each with multiple dimensions. CAS is a consensus-based body of more than 40 associations in higher education; thus, these learning domains have been confirmed by a range of student affairs functional area representatives. When we recently provided our division of student affairs with a list of options for student learning outcomes, including using the CAS domains and dimensions, people felt less fearful because they had options from which to choose.

○ **Identify top priorities.** There is a propensity to want to assess everything, but we should be most diligent about assessing things that matter given the context and objectives of the program (which are not always learning outcomes but, rather, program outcomes). With student learning, we can have multiple learning outcomes for a department, functional area, and program, but we should not feel compelled to assess all of them all the time. What matters most this year?

○ **Follow a formula.** Writing is hard! People feel pressure about writing learning outcomes; a good rule of thumb is to use Bloom's Taxonomy for the right verb, do not compound outcomes, and follow a simple formula, such as the ABC(D) model: audience, behavior, and condition: "As a result of (condition), (audience) will (know/be/be able to) (Bloom's taxonomy verb) (behavior)." In some cases, you will want to add a "D" for the degree to which something occurs. This is important if you are concerned with some level of completion across participants. For example, "As a result of attending the leadership retreat, organization leaders will be able to demonstrate competence in applying registration policies in at least four of five case studies."

○ **Measure up.** Any good learning outcome can be measured with some kind of evidence. The evidence might be the results of an evaluation or the documentation of a collection of simple observations of participants. The idea of "evidence" often feels very scary to professionals who view a survey as the immediate answer to all assessment demands. You need to be more creative, for example, the 4-1-1 method is a good way to assess. Have participants write down four things they learned, one thing they will do as a result of participation, and one thing with which they need more help. You can take this information and match it to the predetermined learning outcomes of the program. Knowing what they will do and what else they need to know is great for advising students. (personal communication, May 29, 2012) information sessions to websites to individual visits at high schools throughout the United States (Office of Admission Student Learning Outcomes, 2012).

Auxiliary Services

The Office of Auxiliary Services at Nicholls State University in Louisiana supports the institution's mission as well as the student affairs division's goals and objectives by fulfilling its own 11 goals and influencing five student outcome areas (Goals and Student Outcomes, 2012).

Campus Centers/Student Unions

The Hulman Memorial Student Union (HMSU) at Indiana State University contributes to the division's Master Assessment Plan by conducting guest satisfaction surveys, usage reports, reservation surveys, programming surveys, and need surveys. A report on the measures of student behavior was created after students attended a professional skills development workshop. Specific behavioral outcomes were identified and measured, including strengths and weaknesses (HMSU Research and Assessment, 2012). The Ohio State University Ohio Union used CAS College Union standards and the Association of College Unions International Core Competencies to create desirable student learning outcomes such as intellectual growth, effective communication, enhanced self-esteem, realistic self-appraisal, clarified values, and career choices (Burden et al., 2008). The union's use of tables and specific examples of outcome behaviors is readily transferrable to a working rubric document.

Career Services

The Career Center at Boston College in Massachusetts uses a rubric to assess practice interviews. During a 1-hour practice interview with a career advising staff member, the advisor offers students insights and suggestions to improve their interviewing skills. The discussion is guided by a rubric that defines the skills students need to demonstrate: verbal and nonverbal communication, listening, value of previous experience, and preparation and interest. At the end of the session, students are ranked on a scale from "occasionally" to "consistently." The rubric is used as a teaching tool to add a learning element summarizing the practice interview (Using a Rubric to Assess Practice Interviews, 2012). Learning outcomes have taken center stage at Indiana State University's Career Center since at least 2004. Learning outcomes are used for student internship evaluations and to measure student behavior after workshops and interviews (Career Center Research and Assessment, 2012).

Counseling and Health Programs

The Center for Health and Wellbeing at The University of Vermont offers use and student

---

QUICK TIP

"Dedicate a full-time position to a culture of evidence. The impact of campus housing, recreational sports, and campus activities and involvement is well defined, but having a dedicated staff member to advance a culture of evidence across the division takes these benefits to a higher level."
—*Norbert W. Dunkel, associate vice president for student affairs, University of Florida (personal communication, May 24, 2012)*

satisfaction surveys to determine student satisfaction. The university also tracks the number
of clinical visits (Utilization and Student
Satisfaction at CHWB, 2011). The Indiana
State University Student Counseling Center
created the Counseling Outcomes Assessment
Study to determine whether clients would
report learning in one or more of the 13 counseling behavior areas (Report of Outcomes of
Student Counseling Clients, 2007).

Disability Support

Meredith College in North Carolina created
learning outcomes for students who used the
counseling center's disability services, as well as learning objectives for faculty (Welcome to Disability
Services, 2011).

Distance Education

Ventura College in California keeps it simple with two college-level student learning outcomes:
information competency, and critical thinking and problem solving. Units develop and measure
specific, goal-oriented outcomes. Outcome statements look like this: "At least 20% of the faculty
completing distance education training provided by the college will use one or more teaching tools/
techniques in their distance education course" (Distance Education, 2011).

Fraternity and Sorority Programs

Since 1998, the fraternity and sorority community at Indiana University–Purdue University
Indianapolis has used the campuswide expectations for baccalaureate degree recipients—Principles
of Undergraduate Learning (PULs)—as the core of its learning outcomes. The PULs include two
primary learning outcomes (critical thinking and values and ethics), as well as four complementary
learning outcomes (core communication and quantitative skills; integration and application of
knowledge; intellectual depth, breadth, and adaptiveness; and understanding society and culture)
(Community and Program Assessment, 2011).

Housing and Residence Life

Pathways is Boston College's first-year residential life experience for the 306 students living in
Hardey House and Cushing Hall. The program purposefully integrates the school's mission into a
first-year residential program that includes overall student experience, overall resident advisor experience, Frosh.0 (small discussion groups), resident assistant training, an alternative spring break, and an
academic initiative. Each of the components has an assessment strategy, such as short-answer surveys,
rubrics, focus groups, observations, and other evidence of learning that correlate to outcomes (What
Is Pathways?, 2012).

QUICK TIP

"Establish an annual culture of evidence symposium. Peer
presentations of evidence collected and analyzed over the
course of the year can be powerful motivators for continued
staff involvement, senior management's understanding,
and increased benefits to student programs and services."
—*Norbert W. Dunkel, associate vice president for student affairs,
University of Florida (personal communication, May 24, 2012)*

QUICK TIP

"A director of student housing typically will supervise fiscal operations associated with campus residences—potentially tens of millions of dollars. Clearly, the director has significant responsibility for making sure that the fiscal operation is sound, and that the annual budget is in balance. In this example, an important metric is the extent to which the annual budget is in balance. Moreover, funds need to be set aside so that building maintenance and development can be completed on schedule. Roofs need to be repaired, furniture replaced, technology improved, and so on, and these requirements necessitate having funds available. Paying for these repairs and improvements requires sophisticated budget management; accordingly, each year the housing director will need to demonstrate that a long-range fiscal plan has been implemented and funds have been identified to ensure the viability of the housing operation. The agnostic would argue that unless a budget is in balance and facilities in good repair, student learning would be affected negatively." *—John H. Schuh, distinguished professor of educational leadership and policy studies emeritus, Iowa State University (personal communication, May 24, 2012)*

The Office of Residence Life and Housing at Bridgewater State University in Massachusetts has created a multitude of learning outcomes for programs and services, ranging from general student outcomes geared toward living in a residential community (e.g., *Students will be able to effectively communicate with their fellow residents*) to first-year student housing assignments (e.g., *Students will be able to recognize the importance of respecting the needs of others*) to programming (e.g., *Residents will be able to expand their knowledge to challenge current beliefs*). Additional outcomes have been created for the First Year Residential Experience program, the programs held during the crucial first six weeks of the school year, the Leaders Emerging and Developing series, Community Watch Committee programs, and Residence Life and Housing Sustainability Committee programs (e.g., *Students will be able to identify on- and off-campus resources that promote sustainable practices*). Each residential learning community has specific outcomes focused on its community purpose, and staff members (students and professionals) are provided with outcomes for every step of employment, from resident assistant recruitment, application, and experience processes to staff training. Bridgewater even includes facilities in its learning outcomes, from work orders to damage billing to appeals. Additionally, every residence hall student organization has specific learning outcomes (B. Moriarty, personal communication, April 30, 2012).

International Students

Ventura College helps international students set their course by focusing on three college-level student learning outcomes: (1) information competency, (2) critical thinking and problem solving, and (3) social interaction and life skills. These learning skills are translated into service unit outcomes and assessed periodically. The following are examples of outcomes:

☼ International students will demonstrate knowledge about their immigration status and understand the requirements for maintaining their visa status.

☼ International students will demonstrate success by maintaining satisfactory academic progress.

☼ International students will demonstrate an understanding of the United States by their successful integration into the community. (International Students, 2011)

The W.E.B. DuBois International House (I-House) at Morehouse College in Georgia brings together academic affairs, student affairs, and wellness services to offer an integrated living-learning experience for international students. I-House has established a mission, goals, and three learning outcomes for all international students and U.S. citizens who live there (W.E.B. DuBois International House, 2009).

Internships and Cooperative Education

As part of their undergraduate humanities program, students at the State University of New York Maritime College may enroll in internship hours, complete with learning outcomes. Students must acquire skills in three areas to demonstrate the acquisition and retention of understandings and competencies. In the area of communication skills, students must demonstrate accomplishments in oral and written communication evidenced by daily logs, e-mail communication with faculty, and the clear and persuasive expression of ideas. Students must demonstrate at least six learning outcomes in the category of cognitive skills, which may include organizing and maintaining information, negotiating and arriving at a decision, or working in cross-cultural or multinational systems. Additionally, students must accomplish at least eight professional skills learning outcomes, such as exercising leadership, behaving ethically, teaching others, and participating as a member of a team (Maritime Studies Internship, 2011).

Learning Assistance Programs/Tutoring

In 2006, Brazosport College in Texas crafted a quality enhancement plan called *Creating a Connected, Integrated Transitional Education Program*. The plan came into being after a review of institutional research data, discussions with college faculty and staff, and examination of national research data confirmed that transitional education offered the best opportunity for improving student learning outcomes. To make the desired changes, Brazosport activated the plan, adopted four learner outcomes, and created institutional and program goals to develop a structure that supports these goals. The plan includes assessment strategies, implementation tasks, and timelines (Brazosport College Quality Enhancement Plan, 2006).

Lesbian, Gay, Bisexual, and Transgender Programs

The House of Roy is a specialty housing community at Ithaca College in New York that serves students who are interested in issues of gender identity and sexual orientation. Students who live in the House of Roy can explore and express who they are in the community through learning outcomes built around the areas of effective communication, healthy behavior, appreciating diversity, personal and educational goals, and enhanced self-esteem (House of Roy Learning Outcomes, 2010).

Multicultural Student Programs and Services

The Office of AHAN (African American, Hispanic, Asian American, and Native American) Student Programs at Boston College "Opened the DOR" with its Dialogues on Race program, demonstrating programmatic and student learning outcomes. After completing the session, 100% of the participants understood and could correctly define institutional racism, and 100% would

IN THE SPOTLIGHT

Sandra Mahoney, director of assessment and student development services at the University of the Pacific in California, shares the experience of the Division of Student Life in developing outcomes-based assessment to create a culture of evidence:

Student Life bases its culture of evidence on the Total Quality Management approach to systems thinking and improvement and uses an integrated systems approach to assess for results-based decision making. The divisionwide, inclusive assessment processes give every division member a participatory role in shared accountability for student success.

Challenges and Solutions

When the division began comprehensive assessment of student learning, most programs focused on assessing student satisfaction with a program or an event. On the basis of the results of an annual meta-assessment, staff development workshops addressed topics related to direct measurement of student learning, such as the use of rubrics. Departments learned to commit to direct assessment of students' deep learning.

The challenge of housing student life assessment data over time emerged. Some departments needed to have their student learning outcomes from previous years readily available; other departments wanted the flexibility to create a new set of outcomes for the year. Anticipating a university-wide need, the Office of Institutional Research created a strategic planning and reporting database, the Pacific Plan. Student Life trained its department assessment leaders to use the database, and department directors now share the following information: departmental mission, vision, values, program objectives, student learning outcomes, descriptions of assessment methods, the results of program-level assessment, and the use of those results for formative purposes. The Pacific Plan information is displayed in real time on the university's Student Life assessment web page, so the assessment information and evidence remain transparent and accessible for decision making.

Lessons Learned

Outcomes assessment must become an integrated, ongoing, and seamless part of the learning environment, and must provide important feedback to both educators and students.

A culture of evidence based on measuring learning outcomes that are aligned with universitywide objectives guides students and staff to pay attention to attributes of the environment that hold shared significance.

The intentional efforts to create a highly collaborative environment (cross-departmental assessment teams, in-depth professional learning for divisionwide staff, connecting with campus partners, staying open to new ideas to make assessment a unifying practice) have resulted in unlikely and thus powerful relationships built on shared meaning and accountability for student learning and success. (personal communication, May 29, 2012)

recommend the program to a peer. Additional learning outcomes included the ability to articulate the importance of learning about different experiences based on race, culture, and ethnicity; ability to demonstrate an increased level of comfort in discussing issues of race in academic and social settings; and ability to demonstrate a clear understanding of institutional racism and how it affects society (Open the DOR, 2012).

Orientation

Students who participate in new student orientation and first-year programs at Bowling Green State University in Ohio develop personal action plans related to academic success, career development, leadership and engagement, and personal and fiscal responsibility. Students also must demonstrate the ability to recognize Bowling Green's learning outcomes, understand how the outcomes are connected to their curricular and cocurricular goals, and describe their rights and responsibilities in achieving these outcomes (Invest, Engage, Attain, 2012).

Lourdes University in Ohio offers a simple mission statement for orientation: "Orientation provides new students with information and campus resources to help begin their college experience. Orientation welcomes new students to campus and establishes new connections with the Lourdes community" (Mission and Outcomes, 2012, para. 1). Lourdes learning outcomes require students who complete orientation to demonstrate their ability to navigate the campus, identify learning opportunities outside the classroom, identify campus services, and outline campus rules and expectations (Mission and Outcomes, 2012).

Parent and Family Programs

Parents contribute to University of Minnesota students' success by supporting the university's goals for student learning and development outcomes. The university asks parents to:

- ⚙ Challenge their student to identify, define, and solve problems independently.
- ⚙ Have their student set and achieve personal goals and make responsible decisions in relation to academics, career planning, social interactions, and community engagement.
- ⚙ Understand and support the university's commitment to academic excellence and integrity, ethical behavior, diversity, and civility.
- ⚙ Empower their student to examine personal values.
- ⚙ Encourage their son or daughter to learn about and respect the values and beliefs of others.

QUICK TIP

"A number of services in student affairs are designed to provide quick, accurate services to students but probably do not have learning as a central outcome. Examples could include requesting a transcript, paying fees online, ordering an ice cream cone at a snack bar, and registering for classes after meeting with an academic adviser. These interactions are transactional in nature. They need to be evaluated from a student or other client satisfaction perspective. In my years as a student affairs administrator, we administered satisfaction surveys with students and used 'secret shoppers' to measure how well the services were provided from the 'customer' point of view." —*John H. Schuh, distinguished professor of educational leadership and policy studies emeritus, Iowa State University (personal communication, May 24, 2012)*

✿ Allow their student to accept the consequences of his or her actions and accept responsibility for personal errors. (Desired Outcomes for Parent/Family Involvement, 2012)

✿ The University of the Pacific in California has detailed learning outcomes and assessment measures for each new student and family program. The result is a readable chart that outlines outcome progress, from the stated objective to how the outcome will be assessed to the results of the evidence and what that means to the program director (Student Learning Outcomes for New Student and Family Programs, n.d.).

Registrar Programs and Services

Union College in New York recognizes that all student services areas can create program objectives. The objectives for the Office of the Registrar include: (1) provide accurate transcripts to current and former students in a timely manner; (2) import student schedules and courses requiring final exam scheduling and arrange them to produce a conflict-free schedule, with the fewest exams in one day for each student; (3) process change of major/minor forms promptly; (4) meet with seniors to ensure that they will complete graduation requirements; (5) register students for classes in a timely manner; and (6) collect grades from faculty and report them to students (Assessment: Registrar's Objectives, 2011).

Service Learning Programs

The Volunteer and Service Learning Center at Boston College wanted to determine whether students were learning and developing as mentors in their roles as Big Brothers and Big Sisters. The center conducted personal interviews pertaining to learning outcomes, student involvement, and program operations. The interviews revealed that although participants were enthusiastic about the program, many had difficulty articulating the value of the mentoring relationship. The study authors recommended the creation of more opportunities for students to recognize their own personal growth and articulate it through structured reflection and training (Volunteer and Service Learning Center, 2012).

Student Conduct Programs

Learning outcomes for the student conduct program at Lafayette College in Pennsylvania are simple and measurable: (1) Students will know that policies and expectations related to student behavior are explained in the Student Handbook and where the Student Handbook is located; (2) students will have a basic understanding of their rights and responsibilities as members of the Lafayette community; and (3) students who meet with staff members regarding violations will be able to articulate how their decisions may affect the attainment of their personal and academic goals (Division of Campus Life, 2012).

Student Life and Leadership Programs

Students at Eastern Michigan University can participate in LeaderShape, which helps participants achieve four primary outcomes: (1) increase their commitment to acting consistently with core ethical values, personal values, and convictions; (2) increase their capability to develop and enrich relationships as well as to increase their commitment to respecting the dignity and contribution of all people; (3) embrace the belief in a healthy disregard for the impossible; and (4) develop the capability to produce extraordinary results. In addition, student participants learn to work in high-performance teams; practice decision making for ethical dilemmas; learn to deal with change; clarify personal values and standards; and understand and respect the values of others (LeaderShape, 2012).

TRIO and Other Educational Programs

Grant-supported programs such as TRIO have long had to justify their outcomes and success. Long Beach City College in California shares its intended outcomes, means of assessment and criteria, results of assessment, action taken, and follow-up in an online table. Assessment method categories include pretests/posttests, internal reporting systems, internal audits, and rubrics (Student Support–TRIO Programs, 2010).

Women Student Programs

Learner outcomes set the stage for a three-tiered assessment of the effectiveness of bystander intervention education at Boston College. Students complete a pretest before attending a 1-hour presentation; complete a posttest after the presentation; and are surveyed again 3 months later to measure whether their behavior has changed. The curriculum was modified on the basis of student feedback and approved to fully implement in a strategic manner (Bystander Intervention Education Assessment, n.d.).

The Next Steps

As this module illustrates, student affairs professionals use a variety of approaches and assessment tools to demonstrate the contributions their programs, procedures, and services make to students and their institutions. Practitioners should develop the skills needed to effectively write and use more than one assessment strategy. Exercises 4.1 and 4.2 can be used for staff training and development or for individual practice in creating effective, measurable outcomes and rubrics. As John Schuh observes, there is only one option student affairs professionals do not have: the option to do nothing.

> Student affairs officers who think that they simply can outlast the accountability movement, in my view, are making a tragic mistake and ultimately they are engaging in professionally risky behavior. Regardless of position or responsibility, they do need to provide information that provides assurances to their stakeholders and provides a basis for planning and developing new programs and initiatives or eliminating those that do not work. (personal communication, May 24, 2012)

APPLY THE CONCEPTS

Exercise 4.1—*Assessing Departmental Programs and Services*

The application of Module 4 concepts can be a starting point for assessing departmental programs and services. It may be helpful to talk through these questions first in a staff meeting, with supervisors, or with colleagues.

1. **Ask who, what, when, where, why, and how:**
   - What is the program or service to be assessed? Why? What is to be learned about this program? What is the specific issue or potential problem?
   - How is this program or service aligned with departmental goals or the university mission?
     * Who is the audience? What will your audience learn, know, or be able to do after participating in this program or initiative?
     * Who needs to be involved or be aware of this assessment? How might they be included in the planning?
   - What techniques will be used to conduct your assessment? What further training or information is needed to use those techniques?
   - When and where will you conduct your assessment?

2. **Define your purpose:**
   - What is/are the purpose(s) of this assessment?
     * Reinforce or emphasize the mission of your unit.
     * Modify, shape, and improve programs and performance.
     * Critique a program's quality or value compared with the program's previously defined principles.
     * Inform planning.
     * Inform decision making.
     * Evaluate programs.
     * Contribute data to assist in requesting for additional funds from the university or the external community.
     * Help meet accreditation requirements, models of best practices, and national benchmarks. (Bresciani, 2001)
     * Other_____

3a. Write one program outcome, using the ABCD model:

_____

_____

_____

_____

3b. Is this is an acceptable outcome? Check by posing the following questions:
- Is it clear what you are assessing?
- Is the intended outcome measuring something useful and meaningful?
- Is the outcome measurable?
- How will this outcome be measured? (Bresciani, 2001)

4a. Write one student learning outcome, using the ABCD model:

_____

_____

_____

_____

4b. Is this is an acceptable outcome? Check by posing the following questions:
- Is it clear what you are assessing?
- Is the intended outcome measuring something useful and meaningful?
- Is the outcome measurable?
- How will this outcome be measured? (Bresciani, 2001)

5a. Write one developmental outcome, using the ABCD model:

_____

_____

_____

_____

5b. Is this is an acceptable outcome? Check by posing the following questions:
- Is it clear what you are assessing?
- Is the intended outcome measuring something useful and meaningful?
- Is the outcome measurable?
- How will this outcome be measured? (Bresciani, 2001)

6. In what situation might a rubric be used in place of outcomes?

_____

_____

_____

_____

APPLY THE CONCEPTS

Exercise 4.2—*Create Your Own Rubric*

1. Create your own rubric, using the following template.

	Beginning 1	Developing 2	Accomplished 3	Exemplary 4	Score
Stated objective or performance	Description of identifiable performance characteristics reflecting a beginning level of performance.	Description of identifiable performance characteristics reflecting development and movement toward mastery of performance.	Description of identifiable performance characteristics reflecting mastery of performance.	Description of identifiable performance characteristics reflecting the highest level of performance.	
Stated objective or performance	Description of identifiable performance characteristics reflecting a beginning level of performance.	Description of identifiable performance characteristics reflecting development and movement toward mastery of performance.	Description of identifiable performance characteristics reflecting mastery of performance.	Description of identifiable performance characteristics reflecting the highest level of performance.	
Stated objective or performance	Description of identifiable performance characteristics reflecting a beginning level of performance.	Description of identifiable performance characteristics reflecting development and movement toward mastery of performance.	Description of identifiable performance characteristics reflecting mastery of performance.	Description of identifiable performance characteristics reflecting the highest level of performance.	
Stated objective or performance	Description of identifiable performance characteristics reflecting a beginning level of performance.	Description of identifiable performance characteristics reflecting development and movement toward mastery of performance.	Description of identifiable performance characteristics reflecting mastery of performance.	Description of identifiable performance characteristics reflecting the highest level of performance.	

Note. Reprinted from *Rubric Template,* by B. Dodge, 1996, retrieved from http://edweb.sdsu.edu/triton/july/rubrics/Rubric_Template.html. Copyright 1996 by Bernie Dodge. Reprinted with permission.

2. Check your rubric against these questions:
   a. Is the learning outcome SMART?
      * Specific?
      * Measurable?
      * Aggressive but attainable?
      * Results-oriented?
      * Time-bound?
   b. Does the learning outcome follow the 3 Ms?
      * Manageable?
      * Measurable?
      * Meaningful?
   c. Do you have more than one learning outcome per statement? (Hint: If you have the word "and," you might!)
   d. Do you use verbs like "learn," "appreciate," "value," or "develop"?
   e. Does it focus on outcomes, not processes?
   f. Is the behavior—the learning—something the audience was unable to do before exposure to the program?
   g. Are your learning outcomes wordy and complex? (Hint: If you have to read the learning outcome more than once to understand it, it probably is!)

Answer Key:

The responses to a, b, c, and d should be "yes"; all other responses should be "no." Responses that deviate from this indicate that it is probably necessary to edit the learning outcome.

Note. Adapted from *Boston College Student Affairs Assessment Handbook,* by J. Lackie, 2011, p. 27. Copyright 2011 by Boston College. Reprinted with permission.

RESOURCES

Association of American Colleges and Universities. (n.d.). *Liberal education and America's promise* [LEAP]. Retrieved from http://www.aacu.org/leap

Dartmouth College Office of Institutional Research. (n.d.). *Assessment resources.* Retrieved from http://www.dartmouth.edu/~oir/assessmenteval/tools

Feder, A., Burris Hester, E., Sanders, J., Whitmore, J, & Teresia, G. (2011, March). *Progressive assessment: Thinking beyond the survey* [PDF document]. Retrieved from http://studentlife.lsu.edu/sites/studentlife.lsu.edu/files/attachments/NASPA%202011%20Presentation.pdf

Higher Learning Commission. (n.d.). Retrieved from http://www.ncahlc.org

Keeling, R. P. (Ed.). (2006). *Learning reconsidered 2: A practical guide to implementing a campus-wide focus on the student learning experience.* Washington, DC: American College Personnel Association, Association of College and University Housing Officers–International, Association of College Unions International, National Academic Advising Association, National Association for Campus Activities, National Association of Student Personnel Administrators, and National Intramural-Recreational Sports Association.

NASPA Assessment, Evaluation, and Research Knowledge Community. (n.d.). Retrieved from http://www.naspa.org/kc/saaer/default.cfm

National Institute for Learning Outcomes Assessment. (n.d.). Retrieved from http://www.learningoutcomeassessment.org

National Survey of Student Engagement. (n.d.). Retrieved from http://nsse.iub.edu/index.cfm

Rubrics on the Internet: A Selection of Twenty-Two Possibly Helpful Sites. (n.d.). Retrieved from http://www.odu.edu/ao/ira/assessment/toolbox/Rubrics_Prompts_files/RubricsontheInternet.pdf

UniLOA. (n.d.). Retrieved from http://www.measuringbehaviors.com

REFERENCES

ACCESS to Success First Year Initiatives. (2011). Retrieved from http://www4.uwm.edu/acad_aff/access/firstyr/advising/ceas.cfm

Assessment Continuum. (2010). Retrieved from http://www.uvm.edu/~dos/assessment/Academic_Support_Programs.pdf

Assessment: Registrar's Objectives. (2011). Retrieved May 14, 2012, from http://www.union.edu/Resources/Campus/assessment/outcomes/academicaffairs/registrar.php

Bloom, B. S. (1956). *Taxonomy of educational objectives, handbook 1: Cognitive domain.* New York, NY: David McKay.

Brazosport College Quality Enhancement Plan: Creating a Connected, Integrated Transitional Education Program (abridged ed.). (2006). Retrieved from http://www.brazosport.edu/sites/Community/AchievingTheDream/Achieve%20Team%20Documents/QEPa.pdf

Bresciani, M. J. (2001). *Writing measurable and meaningful outcomes.* Retrieved from http://www.ncsu.edu/assessment/old/evaluation/writingoutcomes.pdf

Burden, A., Cunningham, D., Monteith, A., Nesler, C., Pelletier, J., & Scrogham, E. (2008). *Student staff development program synopsis, The Ohio Union.* Retrieved from http://www.docstoc.com/docs/92311300/Learning-Outcomes-Through-numerous-experiences-and-opportunities

Bystander Intervention Education Assessment. (n.d.). Retrieved from http://www.bc.edu/content/dam/files/offices/vpsa/pdf/Bystander.pdf

Campbell, D. M., Melenyzer, B. J., Nettles, D. H., & Wyman, R. M. (2000). *Portfolio and performance assessment in teacher education.* Boston, MA: Allyn and Bacon.

Career Center Research and Assessment. (2012). Retrieved May 14, 2012, from http://www.indstate.edu/studentaffairsresearch/CareerCtrRA.htm

Community and Program Assessment. (2011). Retrieved May 14, 2012, from http://life.iupui.edu/osi/fsl/assessment

Denny, D. E. (2009). Student life learner initiatives. Retrieved from http://slra.osu.edu/posts/documents/oe-slides-june-5-final-2.pdf

Desired Outcomes for Parent/Family Involvement. (2012). Retrieved May 14, 2012, from http://www1.umn.edu/parent/advice-involvement/desired-outcomes/index.html

Distance Education. (2011). Retrieved May 14, 2012, from http://www.venturacollege.edu/college_information/student_learning_outcomes/service_unit_programs/distance_education.shtml

Division of Campus Life. (2012). Retrieved May 14, 2012, from http://studentlife.lafayette.edu/student-health-and-safety/student-conduct

Feder, A., Burris Hester, E., Sanders, J., Whitmore, J, & Teresia, G. (2011, March). *Progressive assessment: Thinking beyond the survey* [PDF document]. Retrieved from http://studentlife.lsu.edu/sites/studentlife.lsu.edu/files/attachments/NASPA%202011%20Presentation.pdf

Goals and Student Outcomes. (2012). Retrieved May 14, 2012, from http://www.nicholls.edu/auxiliary/faculty_staff

Henning, G. (2012). Assessment isn't an activity. It's a state of mind [Web log post]. Retrieved from http://www.gavinhenning.com

House of Roy Learning Outcomes. (2010). Retrieved May 14, 2012, from http://www.ithaca.edu/reslife/specialty/roy/learningoutcomes

Hulman Memorial Student Union [HMSU] Research and Assessment. (2012). Retrieved May 14, 2012, from http://www.indstate.edu/studentaffairsresearch/HMSURA.htm

International Students. (2011). Retrieved May 14, 2012, from http://www.venturacollege.edu/college_information/student_learning_outcomes/service_unit_programs/international_students.shtml

Invest, Engage, Attain: New Student Orientation and First Year Programs. (2012). Retrieved May 14, 2012, from http://www.bgsu.edu/offices/newstudent

Keeling, R. P. (Ed.). (2004). *Learning reconsidered: A campus-wide focus on the student experience.* Washington, DC: American College Personnel Association and National Association of Student Personnel Administrators.

Knirk, F. G., & Gustafson, K. L. (1986). *Instructional technology: A systematic approach to education.* New York, NY: Holt, Rinehart, and Winston.

LeaderShape. (2012). Retrieved May 31, 2012, from http://216.91.145.118/leadership/leadershape

Maritime Studies Internship, SUNY Maritime College. (2011). Retrieved from http://www.sunymaritime.edu/documents/2011/11/17/Humanities_InternshipLearningOutcomes_111711.pdf

Mission and Outcomes. (2012). Retrieved May 14, 2012, from http://www.lourdes.edu/Home/CampusLife/NewStudentOrientation/MissionandOutcomes.aspx

Morehouse College W.E.B. DuBois International House. (2009). Retrieved May 14, 2012, from http://www.nyu.edu/frn/publications/challenge.as.opportunity/Mukenge.Wade.Livingston.html

Office of Admission Student Learning Outcomes, Pitzer College. (2012). Retrieved May 14, 2012, from http://www.pitzer.edu/admission/slo.asp

Open the DOR: Dialogues on Race. (2012). Retrieved May 14, 2012, from http://www.bc.edu/content/dam/files/offices/vpsa/pdf/Dialogues.pdf

Palomba, C. A., & Banta, T. W. (1999). *Assessment essentials: Planning, implementing, and improving assessment in higher education.* San Francisco, CA: Jossey-Bass.

Report of Outcomes of Student Counseling Clients Using the Counseling Outcomes Assessment Study (COAS). (2007). Retrieved from http://www.indstate.edu/studentaffairsresearch/CounselingCenterSLOReport.pdf

Rubric Template. (n.d.). Retrieved from http://edweb.sdsu.edu/triton/july/rubrics/rubric_template.html

Schuh, J. H., & Upcraft, M. L. (2001). *Assessment practice in student affairs: An applications manual.* San Francisco, CA: Jossey-Bass.

Student Learning Outcomes for New Student and Family Programs. (n.d.). Retrieved May 14, 2012, from https://secure.pacific.edu/planningandresearch/pacificplan/view_lap_detail.asp?PROGRAM_KEY=SL-SLAI&ACAD_YEAR_KEY=1112&VIEW_KEY=SL-NSFP

Student Support–TRIO Programs. (2010). Retrieved from http://www.lbcc.edu/ProgramReview/documents/TRIO_AssessPlan_2010-11.pdf

Upcraft, M. L., & Schuh, J. H. (1996). *Assessment in student affairs: A guide for practitioners.* San Francisco, CA: Jossey-Bass.

Using a Rubric to Assess Practice Interviews. (2012). Retrieved from http://www.bc.edu/content/dam/files/offices/vpsa/pdf/Career.pdf

Utilization and Student Satisfaction at the Center for Health and Wellbeing (CHWB). (2011). Retrieved from http://www.uvm.edu/~dos/assessment/CHWB.pdf

Volunteer and Service Learning Center. (2012). Retrieved from http://www.bc.edu/content/dam/files/offices/vpsa/pdf/VSLC.pdf

Welcome to Disability Services. (2011). Retrieved May 14, 2012, from http://www.meredith.edu/students/counsel/disability

What Is Pathways? (2012). Retrieved from http://www.bc.edu/content/dam/files/offices/vpsa/pdf/Pathways.pdf

Witt, J. (n.d.). *Writing student learning outcomes for student affairs programs and services.* Retrieved from http://assessment.tamu.edu/resources/conf_2009_presentations/Witt_Writing_Learning_Outcomes.pdf

MODULE 5

Applying Various Assessment Approaches to Gather Credible, Usable Data

Andrew F. Wall

THE USE OF DATA IN ASSESSMENT is central to developing a culture of evidence in student affairs practice (Keeling, Wall, Underhile, & Dungy, 2008; Schuh, 2008). The ability of student affairs professionals to use data is often determined by the credibility and utility they perceive in the information gathered through assessment processes (Wall, 2011). Credibility refers to the belief in the quality or believability of the data by those who have a vested interest, while utility refers to whether the data are seen to have meaning for informing change or action (Cronbach et al., 1980; Patton, 2008).

This module offers a fresh perspective on the origins and importance of assessment and research in student affairs and outlines four approaches to data collection: traditional research, action research, traditional assessment strategies, and authentic assessment strategies. First, the module frames the selection of data collection approaches and methods as responses to the needs of stakeholders. Second, it defines and provides examples of each of these terms in relation to each other. Third, the module outlines a model with six domains of practice as a way of illustrating how learning about assessment must involve weaving together technical understanding and practical experience. In addition to describing examples of assessment and research in action, the module provides a model for developing competence that frames assessment as a critically reflexive dialogue.

WHY USE VARIOUS DATA GATHERING STRATEGIES?

Developing a culture of evidence means not only gathering information in a systematic way but also using that information to improve practice, tell others about the work, build new knowledge related to the impact of programs and services, and engage in critical self-reflection. To ensure the effective use of assessment in practice, student affairs professionals must understand various approaches to data gathering and select an approach that will be seen as credible and useful. To foster a culture of evidence through the use of assessment, people who are leading data collection and implementation efforts must have a clear understanding of their organization and its information needs (Patton, 2008).

Understanding an assessment situation in a student affairs organization requires understanding the key stakeholders and the purpose of the assessment process. Key stakeholders are those with a vested interest in an assessment process. If the process is examining learning outcomes of alcohol education programs in the division of student affairs, stakeholders would include the people responsible for implementing the alcohol education activities, such as health educators, residential life staff, judicial officers, and counseling center staff. Other stakeholders would include those responsible for and affected by alcohol use by students, such as senior student affairs leaders, faculty, parents, and community members. The students themselves, as the recipients of alcohol education efforts, would be the final group of stakeholders. While an assessment process might not be able to answer the questions and honor the divergent perspectives of all stakeholders, it is the responsibility of those conducting assessments to explicitly consider stakeholder needs as they select and implement their data gathering approach.

Considering the information needs of stakeholders helps those conducting assessment processes define the purpose of assessment as a part of building a culture of evidence. Assessment has five broad purposes in student affairs:

1. To develop information that can be used to improve programs and practices.
2. To generate systematic information to tell the performance story of student affairs activities.
3. To develop data that can be used to support decision making, most often related to resource allocation.
4. To generate new knowledge; for example, seeing assessment as applied research with the aim of creating new knowledge or developing best practices.
5. To use as a pedagogical tool to explicitly enhance student learning. (Ewell, 2005; Hursh & Wall, 2011; Maki, 2004)

Assessment *for* rather than *of* learning occurs when assessment is seen as a way to directly facilitate learning; for example, when people are asked at the end of an educational session to identify the three things they learned from participating (Angelo & Cross, 1993). The act of reporting on three things that one has learned from an educational program forces synthesis toward meaning-making.

QUICK TIP

Be inclusive. Assessment should not be a process that excludes. Intentionally include multiple stakeholders in the process.

Clarity about the purpose or purposes of an assessment process is essential to select an approach that will allow for the collection of data that key stakeholders will perceive as credible and usable. Stakeholder concerns and the purpose of the assessment are also important factors in selecting an effective approach to data gathering. In this way, data gathering becomes a response to information needs rather than an approach in which the assessment tool drives the process. Good assessment processes must be responsive to organizational needs. The selection of an approach to systematic data gathering should flow from an understanding of the information needs and intended uses of key stakeholders.

DEFINING DIFFERENT APPROACHES TO ASSESSMENT

To select a credible data gathering process, assessment practitioners must be aware of the various approaches to gathering data about student affairs programs and policies, and the impact of each approach on students. In general, data gathering approaches in student affairs are derived from social science research, which uses the terms we define here: *traditional research, traditional assessment, authentic assessment,* and *action research.* Three of these terms are approaches to thinking about social science research; authentic assessment is a method for gathering direct evidence of learning in applied settings. Figure 5.1 shows some of the approaches to social science research, including traditional research, program evaluation, assessment, and action research. Social science research has been described as the application of scientific logic and methods to the systematic inquiry of social phenomena. Traditional social science research seeks to understand social behavior and develop social theory (Gall, Gall, & Borg, 2006).

Within the social sciences, multiple approaches and associated methods can be found. Traditional research, traditional assessment, and action research are not mutually exclusive. They employ a collection of techniques and practices that are overlapping, but they use them differently. For example, traditional research, traditional assessment, and action research all use both qualitative (i.e., interviews and focus groups) and quantitative (survey) data gathering approaches. The difference lies in how each approaches the use of these methods in terms of defining quality (credibility), the underlying purpose, how

QUICK TIP

Good assessment practice involves:

- ☼ Identifying the purpose of conducting assessment.

- ☼ Scanning the environment to understand information needs of multiple individuals at different levels of a student affairs department and division.

- ☼ Identifying stakeholders and their information needs. This involves conversation prior to and as a part of the process of conducting assessment. Make sure to include students and otherwise less visible individuals, as well as people in positions of power.

- ☼ Being careful to avoid having one assessment process address multiple purposes. While conceptually possible, it is difficult to accomplish successfully in practice.

- ☼ Developing clarity and transparency around assessment. This will help build support for assessment practice generally.

stakeholders are involved, and how data collection processes are situated toward data use (see Figure 5.1). Approaches to assessment are more than a set of procedures or methods; they are a collection of practices associated with a thought process on how best to apply procedures of data collection and use toward an identified purpose. Assessment practice is the weaving together of technical know-how with practical doing toward identified purposes that meet the needs of stakeholders.

Figure 5.1

Conceptual Relationship Among Different Approaches to Inquiry in the Social Science Tradition

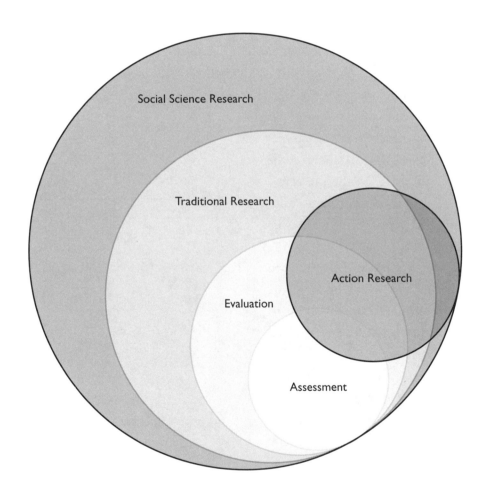

As shown in Figure 5.1, traditional research, assessment (traditional assessment), and action research are interrelated and yet unique approaches to social science research. Table 5.1 provides a series of six categories that indicate places of overlap and difference among approaches to assessment. The table also describes the data collection approach of authentic assessment, which can be employed as a part of the traditional research, traditional assessment, or even action research approaches.

Table 5.1

Differentiating Among Traditional Research, Traditional Assessment, Action Research, and Authentic Assessment

	Traditional Research	Traditional Assessment	Action Research	Authentic Assessment
Definition	Systematic inquiry to explain the social world for the purpose of describing or developing social theory.	Systematic inquiry to describe or explain social behavior and program functioning (particularly student learning) in educational settings.	An approach to inquiry in which the practitioner designs and uses systematic data for the purpose of reflection and decision support to advance more effective educational strategies (Parsons & Brown, 2002)	Method of direct measurement of student abilities under real or simulated contexts.
Methods	Employs quantitative or qualitative methods, or a combination of the two, for data gathering and analysis.	Employs quantitative or qualitative, or both methods of data gathering and analysis.	Most often connected with qualitative methods of data gathering, where problems are studied in their natural context.	Direct observation of individual action that is scored through some kind of rubric.
Purpose	To explain and describe the social world.	To gather systematic information on student experiences; in particular, to connect learning to educational activities and practices for either improvement or accountability.	To study problems in their natural setting as a way to engage practitioners in reflecting on their work and improving their practice.	To examine the abilities of students in practice.
Stakeholders	Research is driven by the researcher, with limited stakeholder input.	Assessment is designed to respond to stakeholder information needs.	Assessment is designed, implemented, and used by stakeholders as co-researchers.	A method, not an approach, concerned with observing student ability to act.

Credibility	Relies on well-established approaches (defined by method tradition, be it qualitative, quantitative, or mixed) to gathering, analyzing, reporting, and judging quality (peer review) of data.	Uses the same approach to credibility as traditional research but also considers what methods stakeholders comprehend and perceive to have value.	The focus is on problem solving through data collection and reflection. Data are credible when they help solve a problem.	Direct observation of student learning through their behavior in real settings means that credibility is achieved through reliable observational practices.
Utility	Utility comes from greater understanding of the social world and practitioners' ability to interpret and apply foundational understanding of theory and social dynamics.	Utility comes from context-specific evidence that provides insight via description into local social dynamics, student learning, or program functioning. Often called "closing the loop."	The focus is on using data and data collection as a part of the process of identifying, studying, and solving a locally situated problem.	A way to move beyond self-report to observing learning in action.

Traditional Research

Traditional research in the social sciences has used both quantitative and qualitative methods of data collection to describe and/or develop theory about the social world. Common methods include collecting survey or objective test data—cross-sectional, longitudinal, or even experimental or quasi-experimental—then using statistical analysis to transform data into information that describes or explains. In the qualitative tradition of data collection, researchers use observation, interviews, and focus groups, then analyze and interpret the data for emergent themes and ideas. A limitation of most traditional research, particularly quantitative work, is that it relies on self-reported data. Traditional research is driven by the researcher or the person engaged in conducting research for the purpose of extending knowledge (as in filling a research gap) or richly describing a social phenomenon or situation. Traditional research is considered to have high quality when the methods (qualitative, quantitative, or mixed) are correctly implemented according to their respective tradition. Peer review and publication in academic outlets (journals or conferences) are well-established procedures for determining the quality of work and for disseminating the results.

An example of how traditional research has been employed by student affairs professionals comes from Monroe Community College (MCC) in Rochester, New York. MCC Damon City is an urban community college campus with a nearly 75% traditionally underrepresented student population. To better understand these students—and all community college students who attend urban institutions—the student affairs staff at MCC partnered with researchers from a local university to develop two traditional research studies in the past 3 years—one on student alcohol use and the other on student experience with the financial aid process. After gaining access and agreeing with MCC student affairs staff on the topics to be examined, the researchers developed questions, determined how they would address those questions, and implemented the study. MCC staff saw the research questions, helped with data collection, and were informed of the results, but their involvement was quite limited in decision making regarding the purpose, methods, analysis, and reporting of the study. In both studies, mixed methods were rigorously employed to gather data that would meet standards for excellence, whether through maximizing survey returns of a carefully selected clustered random sample or purposefully selecting students to participate in semistructured interviews about their alcohol or financial aid experiences.

QUICK TIP

Good assessment involves considering the use of information at each step of the process. Do not wait until the end of the process to think about how information from assessment will be utilized.

Both studies have been or will be reported at professional conferences (student affairs and academic) with an eye toward adding to the peer-reviewed literature in the areas of community college alcohol use and student experiences with financial aid. The utility of the research lies in its rich description of the attitudes and behaviors of students around alcohol and financial aid in the context of the community college. The explicit benefits of the research projects to MCC are less clear, although it is quite possible that practitioners have used the knowledge gained to inform their practice.

The MCC example illustrates the possibilities and challenges of using a traditional research approach to conduct assessment in student affairs. There is a need for foundational understanding of the social dynamics of student life and related student affairs activities in the community college setting. However, using a researcher-driven process that focuses on studying gaps in the literature means that local concerns might not be examined. It is essential to advance basic foundational understanding and theory regarding key student experiences and the related professional programs and policies, but it is also necessary to use approaches that focus on local needs and action.

Traditional Assessment

Traditional assessment builds on the traditional research approach. It generally employs the methods and approach of traditional research, but it incorporates a focus on local stakeholder needs and moves toward considering how to make assessment useful beyond increasing foundational human understanding of the social world (see Table 5.1). The following practical examples differentiate traditional assessment from traditional research. The first example involves the long-running implementation of the Core Institute's alcohol and other drug (AOD) survey in Illinois, while the second describes the implementation of student learning outcomes and template-driven assessment at the Hobart and William Smith Colleges in Geneva, New York.

Every two years since 2000, approximately 25 higher education institutions in Illinois—including community colleges, 4-year public institutions, and 4-year private not-for-profit institutions—have used the Core survey, a traditional assessment tool, to assess student substance use. Funded by the Illinois Department of Human Services, the survey enables the creation of a snapshot of student AOD use across state institutions. In addition, the biannual assessment provides campus-specific trend data on substance use and an opportunity for institutions to do cross-section evaluations of their own programmatic efforts to curb high-risk drug and alcohol use. In this assessment process, each campus works with the Core Institute at Southern Illinois University Carbondale to develop its student sample population and implement the survey; campuses receive a detailed report of the findings (including benchmark comparisons for key data on student substance use) along with raw data for further analysis as desired. Although these data have been used in an aggregate form for research (see, e.g., Wall, BaileyShea, & McIntosh, 2012), the primary purpose is to provide each campus with local information to inform its own AOD abuse prevention efforts. The Illinois Higher Education Center for Alcohol, Drug, and Violence Prevention has conducted training over the past 12 years to help schools interpret and use campus-specific Core data to develop strategic prevention plans to address substance use and abuse.

The multi-institutional and multiyear nature of the Core survey mirrors other national assessment projects—such as the Educational Benchmarking, Inc. (EBI) survey in housing; the Cooperative Institutional Research Program (CIRP) Freshman Survey by the Higher Education Research Institute at the University of California, Los Angeles; and the National Survey of Student Engagement (NSSE) survey from Indiana University—in providing valuable benchmarking and institution-specific data that can inform prevention activities, housing services, and efforts to further engage students in their learning. The projects also provide a rich resource for knowledge development purposes that mimics traditional research in its ability to inform foundational questions associated with student experiences in higher education.

Multi-institutional traditional survey assessment efforts employ rigorous methods (in terms of the survey instrument, sampling, and analysis) to ensure credibility based on the quantitative research paradigm, but they can be limited owing to their inability to provide explicitly tailored information on campus-specific programs or individual students. For more tailored information about student learning, we turn to the Hobart and William Smith Colleges (HWS) example of developing student learning outcomes and related template-driven data gathering. This is another way of implementing traditional assessment in student affairs.

HWS Colleges used traditional assessment to create a culture of evidence in their division of student affairs. They asked each department leader to develop a program theory (Chen, 1990; Weiss, 1997) or an explicit articulation that aligned the departmental resources and activities (programs) with the actual work output (what was implemented and who attended), including short- and long-term

QUICK TIP

Student affairs practitioners should be aware of different approaches and methods of assessment as well as the difference between the two terms. *Methods* include focus groups, interviews, surveys, observations, and more, while an *approach* is a way of thinking that guides your work. Your approach and methods to conducting assessment should flow from the purpose of the assessment, not the other way around. Student affairs organizations should foster the development of skills in a repertoire of approaches and methods to assessment. Work as a team to have competency in different approaches across a group. By working as a team, no one person has to be competent in every approach or method.

learning outcome statements. The statements linked programs with outputs and desired learning, and provided the clarity necessary to create program-specific learning-focused survey questions. Each department wrote five student learning outcome questions based on its program theory; these questions were added to three standard divisional learning outcome questions, providing each department leader with a customized eight-question survey that he or she could use to examine the learning associated with various programs.

Each department leader was responsible for working with the coordinator of student affairs assessment to create and implement a survey administration plan. All departmental surveys were centrally scored and analyzed by the assessment coordinator, and the results were reported back to each department and used for centralized reporting across the division of student affairs. Each department leader chose the program that would be examined by the survey, wrote five survey questions related to identified learning outcomes, and implemented the survey in a manner that would generate the most credible response. If department directors wanted to enhance their surveys with additional questions or additional data collection methods, they were encouraged to do so. In addition, each department received training and a template of procedures for how to implement a focus group, which enabled them to acquire the data collection skills to collect qualitative information if they thought this more descriptive type of data would be useful in improving their programs.

The HWS assessment used clarification of program activities and related goals (articulated learning outcome statements) in combination with self-reported data in the form of locally generated surveys to collect specific information on departmental programs. This process used a traditional assessment approach to collect locally situated information, and student affairs department leaders were highly involved in each step. The goal was to involve stakeholders in designing and implementing assessment so that the data generated from the process would be more salient and could be used to drive program decision making and improvement. The strength of this approach is that it places the assessment process very close to the intended users (i.e., student affairs professionals engaged in daily practice); the limitation is that the data are less rigorously collected (e.g., more limited sampling, surveys that are less validated). However, what one gives up in traditional procedural correctness, one can gain in information that is meaningful for the intended users.

Authentic Assessment

A significant limitation of traditional assessment approaches in student affairs is that they employ self-report measures of student experiences and learning (e.g., surveys, interviews, and focus group data collection methods). Authentic assessment is, at its core, concerned with the direct observation and systematic scoring of the ability of students to do things in real settings (see Table 5.1). The residential life training program Behind Closed Doors is an example of authentic assessment. The exercise asks resident assistants (RAs) to address simulations of situations they might encounter in their work. From noise concerns to an alcohol overdose to a student's emotional distress, Behind Closed Doors helps RAs learn how to work assertively, confidentially, and appropriately with their collegiate peers. Behind Closed Doors is a training activity; it becomes authentic assessment when it includes a systematic process for observing, scoring, and providing individual feedback on expressed abilities in action. Authentic assessments use real-life observations (or as close to them as possible through simulation) scored on detailed rubrics to create data on the expressed ability of a person to apply knowledge to a task.

Rubrics are explicit sets of criteria with performance levels that observers can use to score actions in complex social situations. In Behind Closed Doors, a rubric might articulate levels of performance in how RAs confront their peers about excess noise. The complex social skills of showing confidence, communicating clearly, displaying knowledge of policy, and providing clear alternatives for conflict resolution would all be elements of a rubric designed to score individual performance in this activity.

One of the advantages of authentic assessment methods is that they provide direct evidence of student learning, expressed by behavior in real-life situations. This direct evidence, in turn, creates an opportunity to provide feedback to participants about their performance. In Behind Closed Doors, the rubrics include clear, well-developed guidelines on how to suggest improvement in addressing situations that RAs will experience in their work. Direct observation and the development of rubrics are both resource-intensive tasks, but they result in rich data that directly examine student learning.

The credibility and utility of authentic assessment in Behind Closed Doors are apparent in a comparison of this approach with traditional assessment. In traditional assessment, RAs self-report (via survey or interviews) on their learning skills and evaluate their ability to use that knowledge in their position. However, there is a huge difference between reporting that one can do something and actually doing it under pressure. Traditional assessment might provide some insight into the effectiveness of RA training, but authentic assessment offers the opportunity to actually observe whether the training has been integrated to the point that the RAs can apply it in a simulated situation.

Authentic assessment is an important element in the repertoire of the student affairs assessment practitioner. Observed leadership is far different than self-reported leadership ability. Another example is the observed ability of students to interact across racial and ethnic lines compared with the described desire to do so. Authentic assessment can provide insight for feedback to drive further learning for students and for student affairs professionals who are responsible for providing opportunities for learning outside the classroom.

Action Research as a Process of Assessment

Just as authentic assessment addresses one of the limitations of traditional assessment, action research focuses assessment on solving local problems through a cyclical process of using data to inform professional practice. Action research involves gathering data to investigate a local social problem, using that information to advance solutions, gathering more data, reflecting on that data, and further advancing positive change. The process is ongoing—improving social conditions is not simply an end but rather a process of trying to improve the world. The action research process has been explicitly connected to qualitative data gathering strategies and is described formally as a spiraling process of (1) planning; (2) action; (3) observing systematically (most often qualitatively); (4) reflecting (critically, honestly, and deeply); and then repeating the process. The process is collaborative by design, seeking to involve more and more people, and it requires professionals to open their practice to critique, revision, and re-evaluation (Mettler, 2011).

Action research has often been employed in the classroom. In one example, a student affairs graduate class focused on using action research in service learning. The students used an action research approach to help urban middle school youth strengthen their college awareness and readiness. First, they planned and implemented activities based on their personal and professional knowledge. The activities focused on developing informational materials outlining key steps to college readiness. Immediately after presenting their materials, the students gathered information through interviews and systematic observation that indicated that their efforts had not had the desired impact. The students critically reflected on their work, using the data they had collected, and tried a new approach: new materials, presented differently. This approach was better in some ways but not in others. The graduate students realized that they needed to engage not only the middle school students but also their parents and teachers; this realization led to new plans and new implementation and data collection procedures. The process was engaged and authentic; the graduate students often had to reframe what they thought they knew, but they kept the original focus on making life better for urban middle school students.

Action research uses systematic data collection as a tool in the process of problem identification, planning, action, data gathering, reflection, new planning, action, and so on. It is an approach to assessment that situates data close to practice—data are used to improve local practice and address specific problems. Because action research is so close to the problems and practices of concern, it is highly credible and has great utility in informing new planning and action. Action research should not be used simply in addition to other kinds of assessment; rather, it should be an essential component of professional practice.

DIALOGUE: DEVELOPING COMPETENCE AND A CULTURE OF EVIDENCE

Developing a culture of evidence requires student affairs professionals to integrate assessment into their daily practice, rather than perceiving it as an addition to their practice. Integrating assessment means adopting an approach that is credible and useful to you, your colleagues, students, and the organization. This module has outlined four different ways to approach assessment data collection: traditional research, traditional assessment, authentic assessment, and action research.

Competent assessment practitioners in student affairs employ different approaches and methods in different situations to address varied purposes and diverse stakeholder needs. To prepare themselves to implement various approaches, those who practice assessment must develop technical knowledge of the approaches as well as the practical competence that comes from experience. True assessment competence emerges from balancing technical know-how (related to implementing particular data collection methods or specific approaches to assessment) with the experience of observing, listening, sharing, and negotiating difficult situations that arise in practice.

To illustrate competence in assessment practice in student affairs, the author proposes five domains of assessment practice, connected by a circle labeled "dialogue" (see Figure 5.2). This figure reflects the view that the best assessment practice engages practitioners in ongoing dialogue about what matters in their work. The ability to engage in dialogue—with yourself, as in critical self-reflection, and with others, as in discussing work in meaningful ways—is a central competency of assessment practice. Learning to have dialogue about the strengths and limits of organizational functioning related to student learning is not an easy task, but it is important. Dialogue is the uniting activity of the five domains:

1. Purpose: the ability to have transparent and clear dialogue about why assessment is taking place.
2. Ethics/morality: the skills and awareness to discuss openly how information has power elements, including what is assessed, by whom, including whom, and for whose benefit.
3. Stakeholders: the intentional articulation of who are the stakeholders, what are their diverse needs, and who is being left out of the assessment process (i.e., whether we are marginalizing people unintentionally).
4. Credible evidence: understanding that multiple approaches and methods related to data collection are necessary to accommodate different assessment situations in an organization.
5. Action: an ongoing and explicit concern for the use of assessment processes to meet explicitly articulated goals.

Combining technical and practical competence with dialogue about purpose, ethics/morality, stakeholders, credible evidence, and action results in good professional practice.

Figure 5.2

Domains of Assessment Competence

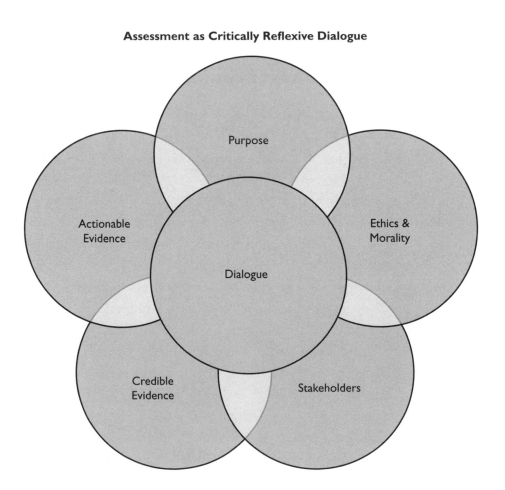

Assessment as Critically Reflexive Dialogue

Technical competence requires the development of skills typically thought of as research skills (data collection or methods skills) as well as skills associated with interpersonal communication, critical thinking, conflict management, listening, and managing one's emotions. Thus, assessment reflects both specific skills related to method competence and skills associated with a broader student affairs professional practice. Research skills are best learned in

> ### QUICK TIP
>
> Good assessment fosters dialogue, not simply data collection. Schedule time to talk about the process and results of assessment efforts.

formal training settings that provide the time, depth of content, and facilitation of learning required to master complex technical concepts. Student affairs professionals should consider formal research coursework and professional conferences and workshops.

Formal learning develops technical skills, but true competence comes from weaving together technical know-how of various approaches to assessment and practical experience in the messy world of student affairs practice. This weaving together happens through dialogue associated with self-reflection, mentoring, and engaged practice. Nothing can replace applying technical skills in practice as a way to integrate technical knowledge with practice experience. Associations and divisions of student affairs should provide formal assessment training, but they must also consider how to create spaces for ongoing dialogue that fosters reflective practice. One excellent approach is through mentoring, where experienced professionals partner with less experienced individuals to support active reflection and learning (Schon, 1987).

CONCLUSION

The practice of assessment is grounded in approaches to social science research, but it must have purpose: Information must be used to improve and support decision making, build new knowledge, foster learning, and illustrate performance. Done competently, assessment can engage student affairs professionals in dialogue about what truly matters. With credible evidence that can be used by diverse stakeholders, assessment provides a process through which each of us can ask ourselves whether we are doing our best work to advance learning, to meet the lofty missions of our institutions, and to ensure that students are prepared to be engaged citizens in a global society. Students deserve our best; assessment can be a positive tool to ensure it.

References

Angelo, T. A., & Cross, K. P. (1993). *Classroom assessment techniques: A handbook for college teachers* (2nd edition). San Francisco, CA: Jossey-Bass.

Chen, H. (1990). *Theory-driven evaluations.* Thousand Oaks, CA: Sage.

Cronbach, L. J., Ambron, S. R., Dornbusch, S. M., Hess, R. O., Hornik, R. C., Phillips, D. C., Walker, D. F., & Weiner, S. S. (1980). *Toward reform of program evaluation: Aims, methods, and institutional arrangements.* San Francisco, CA: Jossey-Bass.

Ewell, P. T. (2005). Can assessment serve accountability? It depends on the question. In J. C. Burke (Ed.), *Achieving accountability in higher education: Balancing public, academic, and market demands* (pp. 1–24). San Francisco, CA: Jossey-Bass.

Gall, M. D., Gall, J. P., & Borg, W. R. (2006). *Educational research: An introduction* (8th edition). Boston, MA: Allyn & Bacon.

Hursh, D., & Wall, A. (2011). Repoliticizing higher education assessment within neoliberal globalization. *Policy Futures in Education, 9*(5), 560–572.

Keeling, R. P., Wall, A. F., Underhile, R., & Dungy, G. J. (2008). *Assessment reconsidered: Institutional effectiveness for student success.* Washington, DC: National Association of Student Personnel Administrators.

Maki, P. L. (2004). *Assessing for learning: Building a sustainable commitment across the institution.* Sterling, VA: Stylus.

Mettler, C. A. (2011). *Action research: Improving schools and empowering educators.* Thousand Oaks, CA: Sage.

Parsons, R. D., & Brown, K. S. (2002). *Teacher as reflective practitioner and action researcher.* Belmont, CA: Wadsworth/Thomson Learning.

Patton, M. (2008). *Utilization-focused evaluation.* Thousand Oaks, CA: Sage.

Schon, D. A. (1987). *Educating the reflective practitioner: Toward a new design for teaching and learning in the professions.* San Francisco, CA: Jossey-Bass.

Schuh, J. H. (Ed.). (2008). *Assessment methods for student affairs.* San Francisco, CA: Jossey-Bass.

Wall, A., BaileyShea, C., & McIntosh, S. (2012). Community college student alcohol use: Developing context-specific evidence and prevention approaches. *Community College Review, 40*(1), 25–45.

Wall, A. (2011). Engaging the professed good of learning as contested terrain. In P. M. Magolda, & M. B. Baxter Magolda (Eds.), *Contested issues in student affairs: Diverse perspectives and respectful dialogue* (pp. 201–214). Sterling, VA: Stylus.

Weiss, C. H. (1997). *Evaluation: Methods for studying programs and policies* (2nd ed.). Upper Saddle River, NJ: Prentice-Hall.

MODULE 6

Designing and Implementing a Culture of Evidence Action Plan

Lori E. Varlotta

IN THIS MODULE, THE AUTHOR provides a personal account of how the Division of Student Affairs at California State University, Sacramento, designed and implemented a culture of evidence, skillfully using the Western Association of Schools and Colleges (WASC) reaccreditation process as leverage. The module outlines the inclusive process by which student affairs managers partnered with colleagues from the Office of Institutional Research (OIR) to develop specific program objectives and learning outcomes; describes the six-step model and template that departments used to conduct and report on their assessment efforts; and shares the lessons learned and key insights garnered from missteps and challenges. In addition, the module reviews how student affairs moved from a vertical approach to assessment—in which directors measured outcomes associated with a single department— to a horizontal approach that measures outcomes across multiple departments. Finally, the module chronicles the story of how student affairs professionals continuously examined and improved their assessment strategies and instruments, moving away from measuring the "simple stuff" toward measuring the things that matter most. A detailed PowerPoint presentation accompanies the module.

SPRING 2005: FACING CHANGES IN LEADERSHIP AND THE START OF THE REACCREDITATION PROCESS

In January 2005, following a national search process, I was appointed vice president for student affairs at California State University, Sacramento. The Division of Student Affairs comprises 22 campus life and enrollment management departments. At the time, the division was gearing up for the second phase of a three-phase WASC reaccreditation process, which, for the first time in university history, focused on student learning outcomes. I was well acquainted with WASC and the accreditation process, having served on the Phase 1 steering committee in my previous role as associate vice president for student affairs at the same campus. The convergence of new divisional leadership and an outcomes-based reaccreditation process laid the groundwork for establishing a culture of evidence in student affairs. Since then, this culture has not only taken hold, but has been expanded and sustained, often at an unprecedented pace.

One of the most significant expectations associated with the change process was for student affairs to assume a leadership role in conceptualizing and implementing a comprehensive learning-outcome-based assessment plan. The multiyear assessment program, launched in 2005, is now the pride of the division and, according to some, the envy of colleagues in other departments. However, the journey has not been totally linear nor smooth, as this overview reveals.

A New Vision, Mission, and Values Statement for Student Affairs

In addition to the WASC process, other "sparks" catalyzed student affairs' transformation into a culture of evidence. One such spark was the revision of the university mission statement in spring 2004, which prompted the Division of Student Affairs to reexamine its governing documents (see http://www.csus.edu/about/mission.html).

I circulated the revised university mission to engage the directors in a spring 2005 conversation about the division's mission. (Before I assumed the vice presidency, the directors had been working on revamping the division mission, but their efforts had been delayed by vacancies in divisional leadership.) In consultation with the directors, I took a somewhat innovative approach toward developing a new statement by forming an ad hoc task force of midlevel, frontline student affairs staff to begin anew the mission revision process. This group of staff members, who provided direct services to students, had a strong sense of what students wanted and needed, and thus what the division should value. This tactic helped increase buy-in from all levels of staff, not just the senior administrators or directors. The seven midlevel staff members, dubbed the "mission committee," were excited by the charge. Within 3 months, the committee had collaborated with staff throughout the division to formulate drafts of the mission, vision, and values statements; the committee unveiled its work with a formal presentation during a directors' meeting. After incorporating some of the feedback delivered at that meeting, the committee presented the final versions of these statements (see http://saweb.csus.edu/students/mission.aspx).

QUICK TIP

Make sure that department missions are congruent with university and divisional statements, so there is explicit alignment at each level.

ACADEMIC YEAR 2005–2006:
FORMULATING STRATEGIES TO BUILD A CULTURE OF EVIDENCE

Armed with new mission, vision, and values statements that delineated the role of student affairs in California State University, Sacramento's future—one focused on student learning and student success—the division began preparing for its continuing role in the WASC reaccreditation process. As steering committee discussions started to lay the groundwork for universitywide assessment efforts, neither the university nor the division had developed a strong culture of evidence. Data-driven decisions were not the norm in most divisions at the university, and student affairs was no exception. Decisions were most often made through trial and error, anecdotal evidence, and after-the-fact reactions rather than proactive strategic plans. Administrators and staff often had difficulty generating data to support or defend their decisions and concretely link them to institutional values and priorities. This reality needed to be changed to help the campus and the division build a culture of evidence.

Student Affairs Takes a Lead Role

In academic year 2005–2006, the university was in Capacity and Preparatory Review (Phase 2) of its WASC process. As part of Phase 2, student affairs was charged with demonstrating the extent to which the campus offers robust experiential and cocurricular programs that result in student learning. In simple terms, this required student affairs to show (in data-driven ways) how effective the division's programs are (i.e., show the value of what it was already doing) and what students learn by participating in them. With strong support from the division and from the WASC steering committee, I committed the division to launching a comprehensive assessment initiative. Specifically, I pledged that

QUICK TIP

At least at first, tie the building of a culture of evidence and the conceptualization of an assessment plan to something big, like the campus's overall reaccreditation process.

every student affairs unit would be able to demonstrate by 2008—when the WASC team came to campus for the Educational Effectiveness Review (Phase 3, see http://www.csus.edu/spc/WASC%20 Final%20Report.pdf)—what students are likely to learn by participating in its programs and how well those programs are responding to student needs.

My colleagues on the WASC steering committee were pleased with this commitment. They were happy to have student affairs take the lead with the institutional assessment/culture of evidence initiative, as most of them knew it would be easier to get the 22 student affairs managers and their staffs on board as opposed to the 1,500 faculty members. Thus, student affairs put itself on the line as both guinea pig and campus leader.

To make the student affairs commitment to developing a culture of evidence a formal component of the WASC process, the following hypothesis to the Campus Life section of the CPR was added: "Student Affairs has assessment plans that identify and assess the learning outcomes that occur in cocurricular and experiential learning programs." When the hypothesis was set in print, only a rudimentary foundation of the student affairs assessment infrastructure had been built, but I was confident that my division would be able to prove the hypothesis by the time the university entered Phase 3.

Revising the Department Mission Statement

With the commitment finalized, I requested as a preliminary step that all directors spend some time researching what other campuses were doing in terms of assessment and reviewing what WASC was expecting of campuses undergoing reaccreditation at that time. Even more important to the task at hand, I asked each director to carefully review his or her department mission statement with an eye toward aligning it with the newly revised mission, vision, and value statements for the division and for the campus.

QUICK TIP

As a senior student affairs officer, be prepared to lead a campus effort by example. Building a culture of evidence is challenging; it may be easier to start the development in the parts of campus that have defined reporting structures and clear systems of accountability, characteristics that may be more prevalent in divisions other than academic affairs.

The departmental mission revision process took place during the fall 2005 and spring 2006 semesters and laid the groundwork for the goals, program objectives, and learning outcomes to follow. During the revision exercise, directors were asked to engage their entire staffs in writing a department mission statement that was directly aligned with those of the university and the division. To ensure consistency, clarity, and conciseness, explicit directions were provided on how to write a statement: Identify the name of the department, primary functions, modes of delivery, and target audience, and limit it to two to five sentences. The directors and I engaged in a back-and-forth process of reviewing the drafts they had formulated with their staff members. The process was lengthy and challenging (6–12 months in most cases), and even now some of the mission statements could be revised for clarity, but it ensured that all criteria were met. The accompanying PowerPoint presentation titled A Distinguishing Mark of a Culture of Evidence–A Comprehensive Assessment Program (http://www.naspa.org/cultureofevidence/MOD6PP.pdf) contains examples of department mission statements, as does the website for the California State University, Sacramento, Office of the Vice President of Student Affairs (http://www.csus.edu/student/assessment/index.html).

By spring 2006, I realized that the divisional efforts could be accelerated with the assistance of campus colleagues with expertise in assessment. It took a single call to the director of OIR to find that support. From that point forward, the OIR director and one of his senior analysts became partners in the student affairs endeavor. Together they worked on the student affairs assessment plan and began presenting workshops on their emerging partnership. They made their first presentation at the annual WASC conference in spring 2006.

ACADEMIC YEAR 2006–2007, YEAR 1: THE DIRECTORS GET STARTED

The assessment cycle truly began in academic year 2006–2007. This was the first year in which the cycle was completed and a report was submitted.

Department Planning Goals

After the directors had finalized their mission statements, I asked each one to formulate three to five broad planning goals that would guide their department's work over the next 3 to 5 years. The directors took different approaches to formulating their goals but were again encouraged to engage their staffs in the process (see the PowerPoint presentation at http://www.naspa.org/cultureofevidence/MOD6PP.pdf).

On-campus and Off-campus Partnerships: OIR and UCF

I first asked OIR staff to help with the formulation of department goals and then tapped their expertise in formulating outcomes. For several reasons, both pragmatic and political, bringing OIR to the table was a positive move. First, it increased the pace at which work got done, since it placed two experts at the division's service. Second, it showed the campus that a culture of evidence must be cultivated through cross-divisional commitments and partnerships. Third, it demonstrated that the evolving image of the new student affairs would be shaped by people both within and beyond the division. Fourth, the partnership leveraged OIR's support and positioned both OIR and student affairs to sing the praises of the teamwork. All these factors not only made student affairs and OIR look good but made staff members feel good and do well.

QUICK TIP

Allow plenty of time for mission statement development, but hold staff accountable for meeting deadlines at different points in the process. Mission statements are brief, but the writing process can be time-consuming.

Around this time, I initiated another important partnership, this one with colleagues from another campus. After attending an assessment conference in July 2006, I invited colleagues from the University of Central Florida (UCF) who had presented at the conference to deliver a two-and-a-half day assessment workshop at California State University, Sacramento.

The Six-step Assessment Model and Template

Together with colleagues from OIR and UCF, I introduced the student affairs directors to a six-step assessment model fashioned on materials from UCF. The steps were (1) mission, (2) goals, (3) program objectives/learning outcomes, (4) measures, (5) results, and (6) conclusions. This model was formulated into a template that all directors were required to work from as they fleshed out their emerging assessment plans (see http://www.csus.edu/student/assessment/images/regions/document/2006ap.pdf).

At first, the directors balked at the regimented approach, but they soon realized that the easy-to-follow template was a highly useful tool (even if early versions of plans were rather lackluster). The template helped uniformly guide the assessment plans and prompted a very consistent approach to actually doing assessment. When the directors were given the chance several years later to revise the template or create a new one, all of them gravitated back toward the original (although the current reporting template has evolved somewhat).

Learning Outcomes and Program Objectives

Writing broad planning goals seemed relatively easy, but writing measureable objectives and outcomes did not. The first step was to help directors differentiate between program objectives and student learning outcomes. The former are related to program improvement around issues such as timeliness, efficiency, and participant satisfaction. The latter address what a student learns or how a student changes by participating in a program or using a service. The directors worked with the consulting colleagues from UCF at the fall 2006 workshop to formulate their emerging outcomes and consider how they would measure them. During the workshop, all units reviewed their two or three overarching planning goals and their three or four program objectives and student learning outcomes with the consultants; at this point in the process, every department was required to have at least one student learning outcome. Before the directors left the workshop, they had completed Steps 1 through 3 on the template (mission, goals, and objectives/outcomes). During the workshops, the directors were encouraged to consult the Council for the Advancement of Standards in Higher Education guidelines as they formulated their initial goals and outcomes. At the workshop's concluding session, the directors were instructed to spend the early part of the fall semester working on the next steps of the template (methods, results, and conclusions) with me and the OIR research partners.

After the workshop, the student affairs directors decided that their student learning focus supplemented rather than supplanted the emphases on student satisfaction and program improvement that had been prominent throughout the 1990s. The emerging planning and assessment program focused on all three areas (student satisfaction, program improvement, and student learning) so that half of the three or four departmental objectives/outcomes were based on student learning (with an eye toward WASC), and the remaining objectives targeted student satisfaction or program improvement. It took most of the directors about 6 months to determine the appropriate balance of program improvement and student learning objectives/outcomes, and then to write all the objectives or outcomes in ways that were SMART (specific, measurable, aggressive yet attainable, results-oriented, and timely) (see Module 3).

QUICK TIP

Tap the expertise of internal and external colleagues. Reach out to campus partners who may have experience in gathering, reporting, and analyzing data. Identify top-notch assessment experts beyond the campus and ask their permission to draw from relevant resources.

Test Run

Finally, as part of the just-get-started year, each director was required to complete a test run of a single outcome or objective and follow

it through the entire process: developing an instrument to assess the outcome, gathering data, analyzing the data, drawing conclusions, and writing it up in the report template. By the end of Year 1, every director had completed the whole process for at least one outcome, from conceptualization to assessment to reporting. Although the data collection and analysis were rudimentary in most cases, the directors experienced the complete assessment cycle, with the accompanying sense of achievement.

> ## QUICK TIP
>
> Early in the culture of evidence process, rather than asking directors to complete a report with multiple outcomes and objectives, ask them to follow one outcome through the whole cycle and write it up in the reporting template.

Wrapping Up Year 1

After completing the test cycle, all directors uploaded their first year-end assessment report to the student affairs website, which started the annual trend of publicly posting these reports. The directors' annual evaluations noted that they had successfully completed the Year 1 assessment activities; however, they were not held accountable for actually achieving the outcomes delineated in Round 1 of the cycle. The primary expectation set and met for the first cycle was to get started. To cap off a very productive Year 1, I presented and co-presented the division's early trials and triumphs at several regional, national, and international meetings and published a short piece in *Student Affairs Today* (see Varlotta, 2007).

ACADEMIC YEAR 2007–2008, YEAR 2: DIRECT AND INDIRECT MEASURES OF STUDENT LEARNING

During Year 2 of the assessment cycle, the directors took a close look at exactly what they had measured the previous year and came to two important realizations. First, most of them realized that they had formulated their Year 1 outcomes in ways that led to indirect rather than direct measures. Indirect measures reflect students' *perceptions* of what they have learned, whereas direct measurements reflect demonstrated *outcomes* (see the PowerPoint presentation at http://www.naspa.org/cultureofevidence/MOD6PP.pdf). To remedy this, several directors transformed their self-reported survey tools into pre- and posttests that generated direct measures of learning outcomes and, thus, helped reveal what students actually learned by participating in the program.

Second, the directors began to realize that the things that matter most are often the most difficult to measure. Early pre- and posttest instruments typically included the types of questions that touch on very basic aspects of the program or service being assessed. With these types of instruments, students' scores demonstrate (at best) short-term knowledge acquisition about a fairly simple, discrete point or fact. Such questions do not reveal whether long-term learning or behavior change is taking place. For example, it is much easier to measure whether student athletes have "learned" about (i.e., can recall or recite) National Collegiate Athletic Association compliance rules than to measure the extent

QUICK TIP

The senior student affairs officer needs to set the expectation that everyone must "just get started." Especially in the early phases, the processes will be imperfect, but the senior student affairs officer must make the call to just do it, and he or she must do it as well.

to which they learn and model teamwork and good sportsmanship. Most educators will probably agree that the latter is more important than the former.

The following example illustrates two important points: (1) how to move from indirect, self-reported measures to more direct measures of student learning; and (2) what can happen if directors, staff, and student assistants do not understand the difference between assessment processes and performance evaluations.

During summer 2006, orientation staff rewrote their assessment instrument in an attempt to augment the indirect satisfaction data they had been collecting with direct student learning data. Before the rewrite, the test was mainly based on self-reported satisfaction (e.g., "True/False: I understand how a student can drop a class"). When questions are posed in this way, the answers reflect only a perceived increase in knowledge or understanding, which is an indirect measure of student learning. To directly measure student learning, orientation staff added multiple choice and fill-in-the-blank questions that prompted participants to reveal what they had actually learned (e.g., "List the three ways a student can successfully drop a class").

Orientation leaders administered the assessment instrument before the orientation started and after the last session concluded. Normally, researchers expect to see lower scores on pretests and higher scores on posttests. Curiously, in summer 2006, the data showed that the vast majority of orientation attendees scored very high on both the pre- and posttest—as if they already knew a lot about the subject matter, and the workshop didn't teach them much. After scrutinizing the data, the director spoke with the orientation leaders (student employees), who admitted that they had coached the attendees on both tests because they believed (erroneously, of course) that attendee test scores would have an impact on their performance evaluations. They thought that if their attendees' scores were low, their continued employment could be at risk. Clearly, the philosophy, strategy, and purpose of assessment had not been communicated to the orientation leaders who were administering this assessment. Regrettably, neither the orientation director nor her supervisors realized that there was mounting (but unfounded) fear about job security. When the situation came to light, the orientation director brought the student leaders more fully into the assessment loop and gave them appropriate training.

The next year's data (summer 2007) looked very different: Posttest scores were much higher than pretest scores, suggesting that the orientation attendees had retained much of the information that had been presented. The misunderstanding at the core of this example provided a valuable lesson from which the entire division benefited.

Wrapping Up Year 2

During Year 2 of the process, the division's comprehensive assessment program started to incorporate more direct measures of student learning, but it continued to rely on a vertical approach to this measurement. While all the departments were assessing key programs and services, they did so from a departmental perspective. That is, the directors examined programs only within their own department, and there was no mutual planning for or measurement of any cross-departmental outcomes. Some of the directors' annual evaluations (depending on which division leader conducted the review) included a brief comment or two about the extent to which they had engaged in the assessment program, but they were not yet held accountable for actually attaining the outcomes they set out to achieve. Finally, as part of a continued effort to publicize their efforts and reach colleagues beyond the campus, two directors and I presented Year 2 processes and findings at the annual WASC meeting following the completion of the 2007–2008 cycle.

ACADEMIC YEAR 2008–2009, YEAR 3: DIRECT AND HORIZONTAL MEASURES OF STUDENT LEARNING

Year 3 was important for at least two reasons. First, it was the year when directors moved even closer to direct measures of student learning outcomes. Second, it was the year when several directors noticed the limitations of vertical assessment and began to develop an interest in horizontal assessment. Both developments prompted directors to significantly refine or completely redesign their instruments.

Limits of a Vertical Approach to Assessment

Although great strides had been made, the assessment cycle was far from routine during Year 3, as nearly every department continued to refine its processes and instruments. Amid the adjustments, some directors expressed a new (and justifiable) concern about continuing with an exclusively vertical assessment. Those directors realized that the regimented process and reporting template all but required such an approach: The design of the process and its corollary tools prompted each department to examine only its own programs and services or determine what students learned by accessing them. Recognizing that some learning outcomes (e.g., those related to leadership, student employment, and wellness) are best examined by multiple departments, they wanted to attempt to formulate some cross-departmental or horizontal assessment measures.

At the same time, the senior analyst from OIR, who had been a strong partner, retired. Luckily, she agreed to come back to the university and work with student affairs as a part-time assessment coordinator via the retired annuitant program. Her first assignment in this new role was to work with several midlevel staff to form the Horizontal Assessment Team (HAT). The team came together quickly and began to conceptualize outcomes that both spanned departments and benchmarked student experiences at California State University, Sacramento, against those of students at other universities. One of HAT's initial and very substantial efforts was to register the Student Organizations and Leadership office at California State University,

QUICK TIP

Let directors know it is okay—especially at first—if they cannot measure the things that matter most.

Sacramento, in a multi-institutional study of leadership organized by the National Clearinghouse for Leadership Programs at the University of Maryland (see http://www.nclp.umd.edu). Participation in this national survey proved to be the basis for important improvements later (see Revitalization Efforts: The Student Affairs Assessment Committee below).

Wrapping Up Year 3

Although the division had been producing assessment reports since 2006–2007, it had completed only two full assessment cycles, and the directors were still being held accountable only for getting started and collecting data. As in Year 2, directors had to show that they were measuring what they set out to measure, but they were not penalized for failing to reach the goal or outcome delineated in the plan. Although some directors began to think about cross-departmental assessment in Year 3, they were primarily in the conceptualization rather than implementation phase. Participation in the national survey was the one concrete step they took in that direction—this participation ultimately shaped the efforts in horizontal assessment carried out in Year 5.

QUICK TIP

The senior student affairs officer should differentiate very clearly between assessment and performance evaluation at the onset of the process, in ways that staff throughout the division hear and believe.

I continued to publish—sometimes with the assessment coordinator—articles that described the division's challenges and successes. In Year 4, I finished a case study of the assessment efforts to date at California State University, Sacramento (see Varlotta, 2009), and wrote a how-to article on implementing a comprehensive student affairs assessment program (see Castillon & Varlotta, 2009).

ACADEMIC YEAR 2009–2010, YEAR 4: USING THE FISCAL CRISIS TO LINK ASSESSMENT TO BUDGETING

By Year 4, the emphasis in most directors' assessment reports had finally shifted to direct measures. Although many directors were still measuring students' short-term acquisition of facts, figures, and perspectives rather than their long-term understanding of substantive ideas or content, each cycle moved the program in the right direction. As directors did their best to continue with what was becoming "assessment business as usual," they were growing concerned about the budget situation for the next year. The looming budget call created a palpable tension among managers.

The assessment efforts described in this module can position a student affairs division (and an entire campus) well in a reaccreditation process. Toward that end, the division was using the assessment data it collected primarily to assess student learning; this was a nod to WASC reaccreditation requirements.

However, assessment and its corollary outcomes can be used in any number of strategic ways, and it is vital for senior student affairs officers to leverage them in the best possible way in a given situation. For example, the budget crisis in California and in the state's university system prompted me to use assessment data to substantiate a necessary (but untimely) budget request for additional staff. Fearing that student affairs departments might become a target for cuts at the very time they needed more staff, I asked myself how I could show that my division needed additional resources to support the academic mission and help the university meet its priorities. To answer this question, we generated and used workload data to show that if the division's baseline were not augmented, even during these very trying times, the essential services it provided would be so negatively affected that the university itself would not be able to meet the goals it had set for student recruitment, retention, and graduation.

Assessment as Part of a Budget Call: Workload Estimators

One of the primary instruments I used to build the case for the division's allocation needs was workload estimators. In student affairs, workload estimators can be used to reflect how long it reasonably takes to complete a unique activity (e.g., reviewing an admission application). The estimated time spent on each activity (in this case, 30 minutes of review time per application) is multiplied by the total number of assignments that must be completed during a specific period (in this example, the overall number of admission applications that must be evaluated during the priority filing months). The resulting total reveals to managers how many staff hours are needed to assess applications and make acceptance and denial decisions. The hours can then be used to predict how many admission counselors will be needed to complete the job in the allotted time.

Workload estimators can be especially crucial during tough budget cycles, when allocations are likely to be reduced. In lean times, workload estimators can be used to corroborate the need to maintain or even increase current staffing levels. During the economic recession, student affairs used workload estimators and other assessment instruments to show the division's significant salary deficit, which would worsen considerably if it took any baseline reduction. The data generated by these instruments were so compelling that student affairs was able to secure from the University Budgeting Advisory Committee 27 new positions in key processing areas such as Financial Aid, Academic Advising, and the Registrar's Office, at a time when other offices were facing drastic reductions.

Assessment as Part of Program Improvement: Student Health and Counseling Services

In Year 4, most directors had a small inventory of data that shed some light on basic office functions; however, the data from two major departments—Student Health Services (SHS) and Psychological Counseling Services (PCS)—were still very thin. The anecdotal evidence from the departments (which were completely separate at this time) suggested that both had a way to go in terms of providing the types of programs and seeing the number of students expected among comparable collegiate centers.

To move the centers in the right direction, a national search was launched for a senior health administrator who could function as a change agent in the SHS area. The top candidate was a professional with no college health experience but extensive experience in both private and community health care. Shortly after the new executive director came on board, she began asking her medical providers basic questions about the number of patients they were seeing per day/week, utilization rates (percentage of overall student population using the services), and cost per visit information. To her surprise, few clinicians had the answers to any of these questions.

Meanwhile, the counseling services were also in a bit of a slump and were experiencing a fairly rapid turnover of directors. For reasons that extend beyond the scope of this module, the two centers were merged and placed under the leadership of the new director of SHS. Today, the two entities are a completely integrated unit in the campus's state-of-the-art WELL facility (a large recreation and wellness complex). The services function under a single name, Student Health and Counseling Services, and students who use the center have a single medical record that is accessed by medical doctors and psychologists alike.

QUICK TIP

A culture of evidence can drive many processes in the university—not only reaccreditation, but processes related to budgeting, program improvement, and departmental reorganization as well.

Within a year of the merger, the executive director was able to gather a great deal of benchmark data, including client satisfaction rates (both at the university and at the systemwide level for comparison) and clinician productivity rates. The benchmark data have led to the formulation of four primary goals: increase productivity for counselors/clinicians; increase satisfaction for all student clients; better identify and intervene with students who are at risk (by having the vast majority of health service users screened for depression during their routine health center visit); and teach students to be better health consumers. Since their formulation, the first three goals have been met according to ongoing data collection; efforts to meet the fourth goal are ongoing and headed in the right direction.

Although this summary of change in the health and counseling areas is short and general, the reorganization process was an arduous one that involved many stakeholders. The data that drove the reorganization and change processes described briefly here were some of the assessment program's most compelling and powerful to date. See the accompanying PowerPoint presentation (http://www.naspa.org/cultureofevidence/MOD6PP.pdf) for more information on the Student Health and Counseling Services Assessment Case Study, as well as the article "Toward a More Data-Driven Approach to Counseling Center Management" (Varlotta, 2012).

Wrapping Up Year 4

The culture of evidence from which assessment best develops can—and should—shape other university processes as well. Year 4 was the year in which it began to shape the way I substantiated budget requests and conceptualized a major reorganization. In Year 4, the directors and I began to demonstrate—in data-driven ways—the value and cost-effectiveness of many of the division's programs, services, and staff. This verification helped the division secure additional resources in an era of declining budgets and successfully integrate programs that had long been separated.

As assessment and data-driven decisions were becoming the norm, I asked both associate vice presidents to comment more substantially in directors' annual evaluations about their performance in the assessment area. However, the two associate vice presidents at the time—senior leaders to whom most of the managers directly reported—were relatively new and did not believe they had enough expertise in assessment or the emerging campus culture to formally critique their direct reports in this area. Thus, despite most directors' genuine efforts to develop and improve their assessment plans, their annual evaluations did not include the thorough feedback and insight that would have been helpful at this point in the process.

ACADEMIC YEAR 2010–2011, YEAR 5: REFUSING TO ALLOW THE BUDGET CRISIS TO BECOME AN ONGOING DISTRACTION FROM CULTURE OF EVIDENCE EFFORTS

Concerns about the budget not only lingered but increased in Academic Year 2010–2011. Despite the fact that the division had secured 27 new positions, there was understandable fear that those positions could be eliminated at any time. Related issues took center stage as vacancies were not filled as a cost-saving measure and directors became consumed by day-to-day management challenges. The initial interest and anxiety about divisional assessment were fading. Staff could not see the forest for the trees, and their assessments reflected the blur. They could not focus on the big picture while day-to-day issues were consuming their time and attention. Their uncertainty manifested itself in stagnant assessment reports; few directors had changed the outcomes, methods, and measures they had been using since Year 1 or 2. While those outcomes and instruments had served them well at the start of the learning curve, they were no longer yielding valuable data. Essentially, the reports had become just another annual job requirement, and many directors were simply going through the motions and checking the boxes on their templates. They were neither modifying their assessment instrument or outcomes nor using their findings to improve programs or services.

A booster shot was needed to help fight the sense of inertia. During the spring 2011 retreat, the associate vice presidents, various staff, retired OIR annuitant, and I provided full-day training for all directors and invited midlevel staff. The retreat was structured as a train-the-trainers program in which senior-level directors taught workshops and showcased their own successes. Midlevel staff members were invited to participate, as many of them implemented and oversaw the programs and services being assessed. Increasingly, these midlevel staff members were expected to help the directors formulate the assessment plan and use the findings to modify programs or "close the loops." Involving midlevel staff increased overall buy-in and added depth to the departmental bench—important factors, as many directors were experiencing staff turnover and feeling a need for departmental reorganization.

Revitalization Efforts: The Student Affairs Assessment Committee

As anxiety over the budget grew, progress with assessment stalled. Thus, I invited several strong directors to participate in an ad hoc assessment committee, which became the Student Affairs Assessment Committee (SAAC). This committee was born from the confluence of several factors.

QUICK TIP

Determine and share early in the process exactly how directors will be held accountable for designing and implementing their assessment plans.

First, the addition of a few directors and decision makers to the HAT. Although the HAT effort in the previous year had gained momentum rapidly, frustration set in nearly as quickly because a lack of senior leader involvement made it difficult for team members to get their ideas off the ground. Second, several members of SAAC had been energized by attending a workshop on student surveys. Third, a desire for student learning outcomes in assessment reports to align with the university's Baccalaureate Learning Goals, which were under revision at the time. Finally, SAAC was charged with supporting all the directors and helping them implement their ideas for measuring what matters.

The creation of SAAC led to several brighter spots in 2010–2011. The committee engaged many staff members throughout the division and, through their recommendations, suggested changes to the assessment process. One suggestion was to completely revamp the old reporting template. In its place, committee members suggested that the division post the assessment report in an attractive, interactive online magazine format that could be navigated via a web browser. Once implemented, this improvement streamlined the division's reporting out function; now, all new student affairs assessment reports are available in this more contemporary format.

The SAAC, in consultation with an associate vice president, suggested adding a new research question step to the six-step model and template. The research question step was added as an explicit prompt for directors to think about an important question to be answered, a skill to be developed, or a problem to be solved. This step helped directors decide on what to study and measure in the first place, which was an ongoing challenge for some. Once the broad topic was identified, managers found it was somewhat easier to formulate an assessment research question. The formulation of such questions guided subsequent steps and helped directors focus on important macro-level issues. Assessments that grow organically out of such questions typically yield more useful results. Naturally, this is the type of assessment that departments value.

SAAC also recommended that the division administer a cross-departmental student employee leadership survey adapted from one used at California State University, Chico. The survey was meant to examine how working on campus affected other areas of student development (e.g., leadership, communication, problem solving). The impetus for this survey were the surprising and alarming results of the Multi-institutional Study of Leadership (MSL) survey administered at California State University, Sacramento, a few years earlier. Student employee responses on that survey indicated that many of them did not believe that their on-campus jobs helped them develop leadership skills or efficacy. The Student Affairs Student Employment Survey was delivered to roughly a third of student affairs departments in 2010–2011, and the results were presented at a student affairs directors meeting. The results yielded interesting insights and were more nuanced and encouraging than the results of the MSL.

Finally, SAAC's horizontal assessment efforts included initiating a pilot longitudinal study of the seven dimensions of wellness, a holistic palette of types of wellness that form core values for the university's health and wellness programs. The wellness types are: intellectual, sociocultural, emotional, environmental, physical, career/financial, and spiritual. The study, led primarily by Student Health and Counseling Services, was structured to compare the wellness behaviors of incoming freshmen with any behavioral changes they experienced as they progressed toward their degree. Unfortunately, the collection of baseline data was hindered by a logistical problem that impeded the examination of the incoming freshmen's behavior. (After the large survey had been completed, it was discovered that the original, baseline data set was irretrievable.) Given the growing concerns about youth obesity, juvenile onset diabetes, and the sedentary lives of many teenagers, the division hopes to resume the pilot program.

Wrapping Up Year 5

The directors started Year 5 at a low point in the cycle, but the changes that were conceptualized and brought to fruition during this year empowered and revitalized many of them. Several directors described Year 5 as the year when they started to "come out of the funk." Their attitude adjustment was fueled in large part by the positive results that emerged from the horizontal assessment and from the dramatic program and service improvements charted in several areas. The area with the most impressive turnaround was the counseling center. The executive director of health and counseling, the clinical director of counseling and psychological services (CAPS), and I joined forces to help CAPS double the productivity rates of counselors and increase the number of clients using the services (see Varlotta, 2012). In an effort to share these unusually strong turnaround statistics with a national audience of senior student affairs officers, I co-presented with the vice chancellor for student affairs from the Missouri University of Science and Technology at the Summer 2011 Association of Public and Land-grant Universities Council on Student Affairs meeting in Jackson Hole, Wyoming.

ACADEMIC YEAR 2011–2012, YEAR 6: MEASURING THINGS THAT MATTER AND TYING THEM TO UNIVERSITY INITIATIVES

With the previous year's research questions in place, the directors began to focus on measuring what matters. This meant aligning departmental assessment efforts with the systemwide and campuswide graduation initiatives that aim to increase the university's 6-year graduation rate and close the achievement gap between underrepresented minority (URM) and non-URM students. Several directors began to formulate more sophisticated and meaningful objectives/outcomes to garner data that will help the university chart progress toward meeting these important goals. Currently, the Academic Advising Center, New Student Orientation, Student Health and Counseling Services, the Veteran Success Center, and the Student Athlete Resource Center all have data that suggest a positive correlation between the use of their services and timely progress to degree. (For a detailed look at these data, see the assessment plans from each department at http://www.csus.edu/student/assessment.)

Wrapping Up Year 6

After six years of going through the cycle, the culture of evidence has become established, and the student affairs assessment program from which it has grown continues to develop. The comprehensive assessment program that grew out of this new culture has triggered several positive changes, even transformations. First, the assessment program helped position both the division and the campus during the WASC reaccreditation process. During the last phase of the WASC process—the Educational

Effectiveness and Review visit—data were used to verify that student affairs programs augment student learning, sometimes in very important ways. Second, assessment helped the division make data-driven requests for budget augmentation and enabled the division to maintain many relatively new positions, even as other areas were forced to make drastic reductions. Third, it facilitated a data-driven reconfiguration and integration of critical services offered in health and counseling. By relying on emerging data to close the loop, the newly integrated department has drastically improved the services it offers and has significantly increased the number of students who access them. Finally, the assessment program has produced data that suggest that many student affairs programs and services help retain students and move them along in a timely fashion toward their degrees. In addition, the directors' annual performance reviews now include a mandatory evaluation with detailed feedback of performance in the area of assessment. This holds directors accountable and supports the significant advances they have made.

I continue to get the word out by sharing insights, trials, and tribulations with regional audiences at WASC and other national and regional conferences, and through publications such as this one. Recently, I published an article that shows how assessment can dramatically improve a specific student affairs department (the Student Health and Counseling Center) (see Varlotta, 2012), and the executive director of student health and counseling services and I co-presented a half-day workshop at the annual WASC meeting. Each time I give a presentation, someone comes up to thank me. Their appreciation is not for the wonderful presentation I have just delivered, but, rather, for my willingness to tell the whole story—the good, the bad, and the ugly—in ways that help prepare them for their own work. I am proud of what has been accomplished thus far at California State University, Sacramento, though the journey has been bumpy and long and is far from over.

REFERENCES

Castillon, V., & Varlotta, L. (2009). Implementing a comprehensive student affairs assessment program. In T. Banta, E. Jones, & K. Black (Eds.), *Designing effective assessment: Principles and profiles of good practice* (pp. 201–205). San Francisco, CA: Jossey-Bass.

Varlotta, L. (2007). VP creates foundation for evidence-based decision making. *Student Affairs Today, 10,* 8.

Varlotta, L. (2009). California State University, Sacramento, assessment case study. In M. Bresciani, M. Gardner, & J. Hickmott (Eds.), *Special issue: Case studies for implementing assessment in student affairs* (New directions for student services, no. 127, pp. 87–94). San Francisco, CA: Jossey-Bass.

Varlotta, L. (2012). Toward a more data-driven supervision of collegiate counseling centers. *Journal of American College Health, 60*(4), 336–339.

MODULE 7

The Role of Faculty, CAS Standards, and Action Research in Building a Culture of Evidence

Brian Dietz and Kathryn Mueller

GONE ARE THE DAYS WHEN student affairs professionals could simply share a few stories about what students were learning in co- and extracurricular settings, then walk away believing they had provided adequate proof that student affairs contributed to the institution's bottom line: student persistence and completion rates. With ever-diminishing resources on college campuses, mandates for accountability, new accreditation standards, and demands for transparency, student affairs professionals must create cultures of evidence that clearly demonstrate the contributions their programs and services make to the institution's bottom line. Anecdotes are still valuable in demonstrating effectiveness in student affairs, but the stories must be supported by data.

> Assessment is an ongoing process aimed at understanding and improving student learning. It involves making our expectations explicit and public; setting appropriate criteria and high standards for learning quality; systematically gathering, analyzing, and interpreting evidence to determine how well performance matches those expectations and standards; and using the resulting information to document, explain, and improve performance. (Angelo, 1995, p. 7)

The purpose of Module 7 is to fill in the gaps and supplement the information provided in Modules 1–6. The module starts by reminding readers that assessment is the core of any culture of evidence and that student affairs benefits when faculty members have the opportunity to both shape and evaluate programs, services, and processes. It explores the role of CAS standards in anchoring cultures of evidence in student affairs, highlights essential questions that are useful in framing culture of evidence initiatives, and provides a link to a PowerPoint presentation that describes how one institution used the CAS learning domains in its assessment practices. The module also reinforces the importance of action research in any culture of evidence initiative and offers examples of how to use action research to strengthen programs and services. Finally, the module outlines the comprehensive program review process currently in place at Orange Coast College (OCC) in Costa Mesa, California.

This module includes additional resources for student affairs professionals who are beginning the culture of evidence journey, as well as those who are committed to strengthening existing culture of evidence initiatives. Most of the examples, approaches, and tools can be adapted for use in a variety of institutions, from small rural community colleges to large urban universities. The important thing to remember is that even small steps move culture of evidence initiatives forward.

CULTURE OF EVIDENCE AND ASSESSMENT

Assessment is an essential element of any culture of evidence initiative. Cosumnes River College (CRC) in Sacramento, California, identified four principles that are essential in framing assessment discussions:

1. Assessment is a collaborative, dynamic, and continuous process to improve courses, degrees, certificates, and programs. It is in dialogue among practitioners that the seeds of true institutional improvement are sown.

2. There is a considerable difference between using data for accountability and using it for institutional improvement. While there is a call for accountability . . . the onus is on the institutions to evaluate themselves to ensure quality education for our respective communities and to place value on improvement through reflection on assessment data.

3. A focus on learning is the goal of teaching, research, and educational leadership. All professionals who interact with students play a critical role in the way students learn and develop as individuals.

4. Assessment is integrated in daily classroom and service practices and not something over and above what staff members already do. The solution lies in striking a balance between making the process thoughtful and meaningful rather than simplistic and compliant while still dealing with the reality of already taxing workloads. (Cosumnes River College, n.d.)

Citing a 1996 Assessment Forum by the American Association for Higher Education, The Research and Planning Group for California Community Colleges (1996) stated that assessment is improved when there is participation from constituencies across the campus: "Student learning is a campus-wide responsibility, and assessment is a way of enacting that responsibility. . . . Faculty play an especially important role" (para. 6). In addition, participation is critical from "student-affairs educators, librarians, administrators, and students" (para. 6). An institution may also choose to involve non-campus constituents such as trustees, alumni, and employers. Ultimately, assessment is a collaborative endeavor, "not a task for small groups of experts" (para. 6).

ASSESSMENT AND FACULTY PARTNERSHIPS

Although this tutorial features several examples of faculty members helping student affairs professionals develop culture of evidence initiatives, more needs to be said about the unique opportunity assessment provides both to educate faculty colleagues about the contributions student affairs makes to the institution's mission and goals and to build bridges between academic and student affairs. Four of these opportunities are described here.

1. **Needs analysis:** Provide faculty members with periodic opportunities (every 2–3 years) to evaluate the importance of existing programs and services and the need for new ones. Inviting faculty members to complete a brief needs analysis instrument helps them reflect on the programs and services required to help the institution fulfill its mission, understand that student affairs is aware of the opportunity costs associated with the programs and services currently offered, and have a voice in identifying new programs and services. The results provide student affairs professionals with data to support decisions to reallocate existing resources or request additional resources.

2. **Process improvement:** Invite faculty members to serve on process improvement teams to analyze, evaluate, and streamline major processes in student affairs that have the potential to affect student enrollment and classroom performance (e.g., admissions, advising, educational planning, financial aid, and course placement). Not only does participation educate faculty and provide student affairs with an infusion of new ideas, but it also gives faculty members a vested interest in making sure the restructured processes work.

3. **Program evaluation:** Provide faculty members with periodic opportunities (every 2–3 years) to evaluate the programs and services offered by student affairs. Inviting faculty members to evaluate programs and services serves three purposes: (1) It educates the faculty about the programs and services offered by student affairs; (2) it provides student affairs with concrete information about how faculty colleagues view programs and services; and (3) it enables student affairs to establish a baseline against which to measure future performance.

4. **Training and education:** Recruit faculty members to share their knowledge of assessment techniques, outcomes, and rubrics with their colleagues in student affairs. Invite them to evaluate the culture of evidence model as it evolves. Recruit them to help with data gathering and data analysis. Ask them for assistance in identifying the most effective strategies to share culture of evidence data with the college community.

LEVERAGING THE CAS STANDARDS

As mentioned throughout this tutorial, the Council for the Advancement of Standards (CAS) has a long history of helping student affairs professionals and institutions of higher education improve the quality of student learning and development by strengthening programs, processes, and services. The revised *CAS Professional Standards for Higher Education* (2012) contains five new functional areas of standards and guidelines: (1) Campus Police and Security, (2) Parent and Family, (3) Sexual Assault and Relationship Violence Prevention, (4) Transfer Students, and (5) Veterans and Military;

and expands General Standards to include technology and distance education. It also revises functional area standards in relation to Campus Information and Visitor Services; Career Services; Conferences and Events; Counseling Services; Lesbian, Gay, Bisexual, and Transgender Services; and Undergraduate Admissions.

As Susan Komives, past president of CAS, noted in her keynote address at the 2006 CAS National Symposium, the CAS approach is distinct in higher education because it sets minimum standards that everyone should reach, offers guidelines that can be tailored to individual circumstances, and provides a basis that professionals can use to gauge the quality of a program or service. Patricia Carretta (2008), assistant vice president of university life at George Mason University in Fairfax County, Virginia, clustered the benefits of using CAS into four areas: credibility, accountability, improvement, and staff development. Carretta also offered seven questions that institutions can use to guide the assessment of programs and services:

1. Is the program or service functioning effectively to achieve its mission?
2. What evidence is available to support that determination?
3. How is the evidence used to guide decisions?
4. What is the impact of this program on students?
5. How are students different as a result of interacting with or experiencing this program or service?
6. What did students learn by participating in this program or using this service? How can student affairs demonstrate this learning?
7. What measurement tools should student affairs use to measure each program or service?

Many student affairs professionals are incorporating CAS standards into culture of evidence initiatives and using data effectively on their campuses. At the 2010 NASPA International Assessment and Retention Conference, Carretta and Annemieke Rice provided an overview of how several institutions used CAS's new learning domains in assessment. Their PowerPoint presentation is available at http://www.naspa.org/cultureofevidence/MOD7PP.pdf.

The University of Alaska Anchorage (UAA) offers another example. As one of its key initiatives for 2011–2012, the UAA Student Affairs Executive Team conducted a full CAS self-study of major functional areas in student affairs. The coordinator of student affairs research and assessment agreed to chair the four-member CAS Self-Study Steering Committee. To build capacity quickly, the committee developed clear processes and timelines, attended the 2011 NASPA Assessment and Persistence Conference, and invited John Purdie from Western Washington University in Bellingham, Washington, to design and implement two training sessions for student affairs leaders. The sessions focused on the CAS approach, building a self-study team, the self-study process, and implementing an action plan for future program improvements. The committee chair built a website that included links to the CAS guidelines in each area, examples of completed CAS self-studies at other institutions, data sources, and helpful tools (see http://www.uaa.alaska.edu/studentaffairsassessment/resources.cfm). The Advising and Testing Center, Career Services Center, Disability Support Services, Educational Talent Search, Student Information Office, Student Support Services, and the Student Union and Commuter Students completed the self-study process and submitted their reports in June 2012.

The remaining areas submitted their reports in August 2012. (A summary of the reports and a PowerPoint presentation are available at http://www.uaa.alaska.edu/studentaffairs/student-affairs-cas-self-studies.cfm.) In 2012–2013, the UAA Student Affairs Executive Team began to use CAS self-study results to connect numerous specialty areas and increase the knowledge base of student affairs professionals, identify opportunities for program enhancement, and build a foundation for strategic planning and assessment activities, including identifying developmental, learning, and program outcomes.

QUICK TIP

"Parker Palmer (1999) describes being stranded on a cliff face and unable to move. Then he remembered the Outward Bound philosophy: 'If you can't get out of it, get into it.' We need to proceed as if we can do this—and we will. Admit what is hard and address it: Begin talking across disciplines; valuing different strategies for measurement; acknowledging the tensions; and unfolding the process." (Komives, 2006, pp. 11–12)

Orange Coast College offers a third example. Using the 2009 CAS standards, OCC designed and implemented guidelines to reduce staff uncertainty, provide a shared structure, and guide efforts to define and assess outcomes. Table 7.1 illustrates these guidelines with examples from the 2009 *CAS Self-Assessment Guides* and outlines the prompts provided for staff members completing the form and the process.

A basic example of how OCC uses data to strengthen services and provide valuable information to the college is the Answer Center, part of the Enrollment Center. Staffed by hourly employees, the Answer Center routes callers to the appropriate departments and employees, but staff also answer questions from prospective students, parents, employees, and the community. Answer Center staff members, who view themselves as both learners and educators, collaborate with colleagues in Information Technology and District Information Services to collect and analyze data from incoming calls. Some of the information collected is basic: the number of incoming calls, how long calls are on hold, and the length of calls. But much of the information collected is designed to help the college learn about the types of questions asked and the information requested. Periodically, data are analyzed to identify patterns; the analyses show that OCC adjusts staffing patterns to better meet student needs, provides up-to-date training for Answer Center staff, anticipates trends, and tracks what students and members of the community are learning and want to know about the college. Thanks to the data collected and the learning that is taking place, OCC has not reduced the staff level in the Answer Center, even in an era of brutal budget cuts.

A final example of incorporating CAS standards into culture of evidence initiatives is offered by current and former Texas A&M University student affairs professionals who chronicled their efforts in *Learning Is Not a Sprint: Assessing and Documenting Student Leader Learning in Cocurricular Involvement* (Collins & Roberts, 2012). A must-read for student affairs professionals involved in student life and leadership programs, residence life, clubs, organizations, or student activities, the book offers strategies for assessing and documenting student learning, writing rubrics for teams and groups, overcoming obstacles, and managing change.

Table 7.1

Rubric for Assessing Outcomes, Developed at Orange Coast College

Program Mission Statement	Intended Student Learning Outcomes for the Academic Year	Means of Assessment and Criteria for Success	Analysis of Data Collected	Use of Results
Cite the departmental or program mission statement.	What will students be able to think, know, do, or feel because of a given educational experience in a course or program? To which institutional student learning outcome is this outcome linked?	What are the specific assessment tools best suited to measure the degree to which the outcome was achieved? What is the criterion for success? How will the college know that the student has learned what he or she was supposed to learn or developed the way he or she was supposed to develop? How will student affairs document the extent of change?	What were the findings? (Remember to disaggregate the data if large groups are involved.) To what extent were the outcomes achieved? In retrospect, what do the data say about the selection of participants, assessment tools, and strategies? What did the data tell you?	How will your area use the data to strengthen a specific program, process, or service? How will student affairs use the data to improve student learning and support in all areas? How will student affairs use the data to support the reallocation of existing resources or a request for additional resources? What improvements have already been made? How will the outcome and the assessment procedures change in the next academic year?

Note. Adapted from *Student Services Program Student Learning Outcomes (PSLO) Assessment Model,* retrieved from http://www.orangecoastcollege.edu/student_life/deanofstudents/Documents/IV.SLO%20Rubric%20052412.pdf. Adapted with permission.

Using CAS Standards: The Pioneers' Perspective

Many student affairs professionals blazed a trail for others to follow in using CAS standards to guide culture of evidence initiatives. Six of these pioneers collaborated at the 2009 CAS National Symposium to describe what they had learned about using the CAS standards. The observations by Bonfiglio, Nagy, Hillman, Tobin, Childress, and Johnson focused on three areas: assessment, the CAS standards, and lessons learned.

Assessment

Assessment is a cost-effective way to benchmark colleges and universities against local, state, and national institutions. It provides student affairs with data to document in a very concrete manner how it helps the institution fulfill its mission and achieve its goals. Assessment enables student affairs leaders to leverage culture of evidence initiatives and build partnerships across the institution.

CAS Standards

The CAS standards educate professionals about the outcomes associated with specific areas in student affairs, thus removing some of the stressors (fear, frustration, uncertainty) involved in creating a culture of evidence. Using the standards promotes a shared vision for excellence in student affairs, provides a common language, and removes politics from the culture of evidence equation. Application of the standards supports the development of new programs, strengthening of existing programs, and reduction or elimination of programs no longer needed. In addition, applying CAS standards sends a message to the college or university community that those who work in student affairs are true professionals and capable of self-regulation.

Lessons Learned Along the Way

Colleges and universities need to limit the number of reviews for campus teams and make sure that timelines are realistic: Evidence collected over a long period can become outdated. Always recruit more faculty and staff volunteers than you initially think you will need. Do not be afraid to customize the standards, if necessary, since customization rarely compromises the integrity of a standard (Bonfiglio et al., 2009).

ACTION RESEARCH

The Center for Collaborative Action Research offered the following definition of action research (Riel, 2010):

> Action research is the systematic, reflective study of one's actions, and the effects of these actions, in a workplace context. As such, it involves deep inquiry into one's professional practice. The researchers examine their work and seek opportunities for improvement. As designers and stakeholders, they work with colleagues to propose new courses of action that help their community improve work practices. As researchers, they seek evidence from multiple sources to help them analyze reactions to the action taken. They recognize their own view as subjective, and seek to develop their understanding of the events from multiple perspectives. (para. 1)

The key to understanding and designing action research studies is understanding that action research is a practical application with the primary goal of program improvement. It is a cyclical process designed to improve the programs, services, and initiatives in a given department, division, or institution. This kind of research is likely to resonate with student affairs professionals, because they tend to be action-oriented and practical people who value continuous improvement as well as reflective learning in both students and themselves. Understanding the value of action research is not a leap for student affairs professionals; in fact, many already are practicing action research, or some version of it, even if the work is not called by that name. This section provides an overview of the concept and components of action research, discusses its importance to student affairs, and offers examples of how action research has been used on campus.

The cyclical process of action research starts with a problem that needs to be resolved or addressed in a particular department, program, or institution. This module expands the concept of "problem" as the starting point of action research and posits that the starting point can also be an area for study and improvement. The following five steps are adapted from models discussed by O'Brien (2001) and Riel (2010):

1. Identify a problem or target area for improvement.
2. Gather data.
3. Interpret data.
4. Design and implement an action plan.
5. Evaluate impact and reflect on action.

An additional step—Step 6—is a return to Step 1. In practice, the cycle may return to the original identified problem, which requires additional work, or it may target a different area. Action research—and the culture of evidence process in general—involves continuous assessment and improvement. Embracing action research means accepting the fact that the work will never be "finished." Institutions, personnel, and student needs are in a constant state of change, which means ongoing work to establish a culture of evidence that permeates an entire division or institution.

Applying the Five-step Model

Step 1: Identify the problem area. This model of action research expands the notion of problem identification to include addressing areas without problems. This is important, because although many areas on campus have high success indicators, they should still be reviewed for potential improvements to enhance student learning.

A problem can be identified by external sources, such as a student who is concerned about a particular issue or another department that is concerned about a program or process that does not seem to work as well as it could. Problems can also be identified internally by staff or through review of direct assessments of students and learning outcomes—obviously, students not meeting stated learning outcomes is a problem. Other problem areas can be programs or services that students are not aware of or satisfied with; for example, complaints about the quality and performance of laundry facilities in residence halls, low attendance at lectures on campus, low knowledge of campus policies, and dissatisfaction with recreational opportunities on campus.

Step 2: Gather data. Once the problem or area for investigation is identified, the next step is to begin gathering data. This step can seem daunting, but institutions and divisions should not allow data gathering to overwhelm them or become impossibly taxing. In fact, as they begin conducting action research, many student affairs divisions discover that they already have a lot of data they can use. Data can come from various institutional sources, including survey instruments such as those produced by the National Survey of Student Engagement (NSSE), the Community College Survey of Student Engagement (CCSSE), and the Collegiate Learning Assessment (CLA). Data also can be gathered through "homegrown" surveys and using existing instruments, many of which can be easily amended to collect additional action research data.

New information can come from focus groups, exit interviews, journaling activities, aggregated collections of reflection exercises, and casual encounters that are recorded and assessed using a previously developed rubric. The point to remember is that the focus should be on how data and research can be used to improve programs. The goal is not to publish journal articles or improve programs at institutions nationwide; the goal is to improve programs, processes, services, and learning at your institution. Keeping this goal in mind greatly reduces the pressure to ensure that data collection processes and procedures are perfect.

Step 3: Interpret data. Many colleges and universities are data-rich and information-poor. Effective action research requires that student affairs professionals analyze and evaluate the data to determine what they mean in relation to the stated problem or area of investigation. One of the most effective data analysis strategies is to assemble a team of faculty, student affairs staff, and representatives from both institutional research and information technology to mine the data, looking for trends and answers related to the identified question/problem. The team might begin by looking through various sources and connecting the dots. Sometimes, team members might have to collect more data to clarify, confirm, or disprove possible trends. This often happens with quantitative data gleaned from survey instruments, when analysis identifies conflicting trends. Getting some concrete examples through qualitative data collection allows the team to place the trend data in context. This additional data gathering can be done through focus groups and convenience sample interviews (e.g., student organizations, teams, residence hall floors, student staff members).

Step 4: Develop and implement an action plan. Once the data have spoken and the patterns are clear, student affairs professionals need to determine how to use the data to address the original question or problem. This work involves identifying potential strategies and solutions, and developing an action plan. Creating a successful plan of action requires a complete understanding of the problem, including what the data reveal about the issues involved with or causing the problems. These findings must then be coupled with available resources and potential solutions to determine the course of action that will most likely result in learning, change, and a positive outcome. The action plan must contain provisions that student affairs professionals will use to evaluate how the elements of the plan play out in the real world. Frequently, additional data collection is required during Step 4 to determine whether the intended outcome or change has been accomplished.

Step 5: Evaluate impact and reflect on action plan. During this fifth step, student affairs professionals observe the outcome of the action plan to determine whether the problem has been resolved. In many cases, there will be a shift and some sort of impact, but the problem might not be completely resolved. This situation might occur for various reasons: The student affairs professionals might not have adequately understood the problem, or new or previously unobserved variables entered the equation after the implementation was initiated. The following is an example of the five-step model in action. It demonstrates the importance of observing the outcome before determining that the problem has been resolved.

Students in a residence hall were complaining that secondhand smoke from smokers standing outside the main entrance was blowing into their rooms through open windows. The institution had previously made the building smoke-free, which required smokers to step outside if they chose to smoke. This solved one problem but created another one: how to keep secondhand smoke from entering open windows on the second and third floors. After some assessment and data collection, the institution decided to implement a 30-foot rule. The new policy prohibited smoking within 30 feet of any building or building entrance; it was designed to move smokers away from the building and the open windows. Surveys were distributed, and respondents said the secondhand smoke had been reduced. The institution thought the issue was resolved until the ground maintenance crew reported that cigarette butts had become a big problem in lawn areas outside buildings. Investigation revealed that when the 30-foot rule was implemented, the smokers moved but the receptacles for cigarette butts remained outside the building entrances or were nonexistent. The institution installed receptacles at least 30 feet away from all building entrances; finally, smoke drifting into windows was reduced and litter was kept under control.

This example illustrates the cyclical nature of action research—how a problem moves from identification through data gathering and interpretation, to action plan implementation, and finally to reflection and evaluation. In this case, the university had to address the problem three times before the original outcome (smoke-free buildings) and the unintended secondary problems (smoke in rooms, cigarette butts on the lawn) were resolved.

WHY USE ACTION RESEARCH?

Action research complements much of the work student affairs professionals engage in on campus. It is pragmatic, practical, and results-orientated, so it aligns with many of the goals and methods of operation student affairs divisions employ on campuses across the nation. In essence, action research involves studying and understanding programs and services with the goal of improving programs, strengthening services, and enhancing learning outcomes for students. Action research is critical to creating a culture of evidence; it enables practitioners to make informed, practical, and effective decisions about programs and services.

In an era of 24/7 communication, unending student needs and demands, limited resources, and shrinking budgets, it is hard to imagine adding to the workload of a student affairs department or division. For many, engaging in action research might seem like a noble but impossible task. An individual, division, or institution concerned about how to get it all done should not perceive action research as adding work to an already impossible schedule but rather as a way to enhance and streamline existing efforts. Action research is designed to identify a problem and fix it. Getting started takes some effort and energy, but the long-term benefits greatly outweigh the time and resources put into the effort.

To truly capitalize on the concept of action research, student affairs professionals must recognize that the process involves more than going through the motions of assessing programs and ensuring that surveys and evaluations are completed. The key lies in understanding and interpreting data, and then using the data to strengthen and improve programs, processes, and services. The goal is to use data to become information-rich.

IN THE SPOTLIGHT

The social programming board at Kalamazoo College in Michigan wanted to increase attendance at weekend events. The board identified the problem as low attendance and conducted a survey to determine the kind of events students would attend. The responses indicated that students wanted access to free feature films on campus. The board reviewed the data and developed an action plan that included the creation of weekend movie nights. The movie nights achieved only limited success and attendance, so the board developed a second survey to identify the problem. Students responded that the constantly changing movie locations and times were confusing and frustrating; they also identified poor sound quality and an unappealing atmosphere as concerns. After analyzing the data and validating the responses, the board developed the following five-step action plan to improve the movie series:

1. Schedule movies at the same time every week.

2. Show the movies in a venue with less seating but improved sound and video capabilities.

3. Borrow a popcorn machine and provide free popcorn during the movie.

4. Advertise the film series with a regular time and location.

5. Change movie titles once a week.

Within a year, attendance doubled; a few years later, students ranked the film series as a top activity on campus. The college now includes information about the series on campus tours and in materials for prospective students. The program board still evaluates movies on a regular basis and reviews the interests and requests of movie-going students. The formula for success has not changed much over the past few years, and the ongoing evaluation has revealed problems (e.g., broken seats and an inoperable speaker). The survey also has been used to provide support for much-needed improvements to the screening room, including enhancements to the sound and video equipment that benefit regular classes as well as the weekend movies.

ADDITIONAL CULTURE OF EVIDENCE OPTIONS

As evidenced by the approaches and tools discussed in this tutorial, student affairs professionals have many options when they are building cultures of evidence. Two important options not mentioned in previous modules are the program review process and the continuous quality improvement approach.

Program Review Process

A well-developed program review process can provide the foundation for culture of evidence initiatives, especially in the community college. The Student Services Division at OCC has had a program review process in place for nearly two decades. Four years ago, after extensive conversations across the college, instructional and non-instructional areas agreed to establish a common annual timeline, a 3-year evaluation cycle for all areas, an annual calendar, and a shared set of guidelines for writing the self-evaluation. This approach provides the college with shared requirements, structure, timelines, language, and processes. In turn, the planning and resource allocation processes are more efficient and effective, as all areas are on the same page in collecting and analyzing data, and identifying resources and directions for programs and services.

All four areas of the college (Administrative Services, Instruction, Office of the President, and Student Services) include peer review as part of the program review process. Student Services appoints a peer review committee composed of staff, faculty, managers, a student, and the college's program review coordinator. The committee provides feedback on the program review document (is it well written?); data collected (are they sufficient, if not robust?); and data analysis (are the data meaningful? is the program meeting its mission and its goals? are students engaged and learning? are needs appropriately identified? are assertions backed by data?) before offering recommendations and commendations.

Student Services completes a comprehensive program review every 3 years. During the other 2 years, programs and services complete annual program reviews that include defining and measuring student learning outcomes, strategic and operational planning, and identifying needed resources. (Exercise 7.1 outlines OCC's program review requirements.)

Continuous Quality Improvement

The Accrediting Commission for Community and Junior Colleges (2011), the two-year college accreditor of the Western Association of Schools and Colleges, provided a list that institutions can use to assess the extent to which they have succeeded in institutionalizing a culture of evidence and reaching the deepest level of implementation: sustainable, continuous quality improvement. At this level (as shown in Table 7.2), an institution has continuous and systematic student learning outcomes and assessment; pervasive, robust, and ongoing dialogue across the campus; an organizational structure that is regularly evaluated and improved for student learning; and an intentional and obvious link between program reviews and student learning.

Table 7.2

Measuring Progress Toward Continuous Quality Improvement

Level of Implementation: Sustainable Continuous Quality Improvement
Student learning outcomes and assessment are ongoing, systematic, and used for continuous quality improvement.
Dialogue about student learning is ongoing, pervasive, and robust.
Evaluation of student learning outcomes processes.
Evaluation and fine-tuning of organizational structures to support student learning is ongoing.
Student learning improvement is a visible priority in all practices and structures across the college.
Learning outcomes are specifically linked to program reviews.

Note. Adapted from *Rubric for Evaluating Institutional Effectiveness—Part III: Student Learning Outcomes*, by Accrediting Commission for Community and Junior Colleges, Western Association of Schools and Colleges, 2011, retrieved from http://www.accjc.org/wp-content/uploads/2011/10/CoverMemoAndRevisedRubric_10-28-2011.pdf. Adapted with permission.

CONCLUSION

Even if an institution, division, or department has not yet begun to design and implement a culture of evidence in student affairs, it is never too late to start. The good news is that many resources and tools exist today that were unavailable a decade ago. As the Resources section in this tutorial demonstrates, today's student affairs professionals can learn from their early-adopter colleagues which strategies and tools yield essential information and which ones lead to dead ends. The goal is to institutionalize culture of evidence processes and reach a level at which continuous quality improvement is a way of life, and the culture of evidence in student affairs is increasingly more robust and meaningful.

APPLY THE CONCEPTS

Exercise 7.1—*Orange Coast College Student Services Comprehensive Program Review Requirements*

PURPOSE OF PROGRAM REVIEW

The purpose of a comprehensive program review and assessment is to make the department more responsive to the needs of the college and community, increase its indirect contribution to student mastery of the institutional student learning outcomes (ISLOs), and provide information for decisions regarding resource allocation. It is an analytical critique of a program that defines its current and future needs to meet the demands placed on it in an effective, efficient, timely, and cost-effective manner. This process is designed to:

- Provide a rigorous examination of services and their outcomes.
- Engage departments in planning program improvements that are responsive to student and community needs.
- Provide information for resource allocation within departments and across the college.

All identified programs will undergo a comprehensive program review every 3 years. Annual program reviews will be done by all programs in three resource areas: staffing, facilities, and technology. Through the program review process, the following outcomes will be ensured:

- Improve programs and services consistent with the college mission, academic master plan, and the ISLOs. Though support programs do not contribute directly to helping students learn, the services provided enable students and faculty to engage in teaching and learning, so the program's contribution is crucial.
- Determine program direction and goals for the next 3–5 years.
- Foster cooperation among college departments.
- Develop information to assist in the allocation of resources.
- Increase responsiveness to student and community needs.
- Improve response to external and demographic changes.
- Respond to state and federal mandates for accountability.

I. Description of Program

Use the following guidelines to describe the program being reviewed.

A. Description and mission of program. Describe the program under review in one page or less. Be sure to include your program mission/philosophy statement and how it supports the college's vision and mission statements.

B. How the program's outcomes relate to the college's ISLOs. Briefly describe how your program links to each identified ISLO: communication, thinking skills, global awareness, personal development, and responsibility. List each relevant ISLO and describe the anticipated student learning outcome.

C. Description of community and compliance influences by external factors, such as state laws, external accreditation requirements, and changing community demographics that affect your program's outcomes. For instructional areas, refer to Title V compliance (California Education Code for institutions of higher education) and Course Outline of Record (COR) revision.

D. Did program meet recommendations from previous program review? Indicate *met*, *not met*, or *in progress*, and provide details.

II. Enrollment and Access

A. Analyze the program's enrollment and/or utilization (e.g., students enrolled, students served, staff served) for the past 6 years.

	2005–06	2006–07	2007–08	2008–09	2009–10	2010–11
No. of students served						

B. Analyze the demographics of the students served in this program. Is the ethnic breakdown of students you serve proportional to the general college ethnic distribution? If disproportionate, please describe known or possible factors.

C. Describe the program's workload measures as developed within the Student Services process. Include budget details. Workload measures include:

1. Budget analysis categories of *expenditures*, as in the example below.

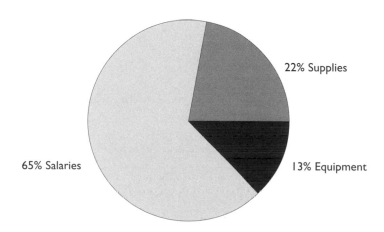

22% Supplies

65% Salaries

13% Equipment

a. List all sources of *income* with dollars and the percentage of program budget that revenue source represents. Please present a pie-chart graphic.

b. List primary categories of *expenditures,* with dollars and the percentage of program budget that each expenditure represents.

2. Provide a staffing analysis including current number of staff, minimum staffing needs, and effect of workload on staffing. Use the prompts below to guide you in this analysis.

a. Provide the program's 5-year staffing profile using the table below. Be sure to include full-time, permanent part-time, hourly, and student assistant positions.

Position	Staffing levels for each of the previous 5 years						Anticipated needs		
	2007	2008	2009	2010	2011	% change from Year 1 to Year 5	2012–13	2013–14	2014–15

b. Explain whether the staffing structure meets the program or department's needs. If yes, please explain. If no, consider the following prompts in framing your answer:

i. Which aspects of the work are keys to the institution's mission?

ii. Has the staff increased, decreased, or remained the same to meet those changes?

iii. Has technology made it possible to do more work with the same staff? Or has technology increased your workload (e.g., adding Internet-based features that need updating)? In what way?

iv. Does the workload have significant peaks and valleys during the fiscal year? If yes, describe.

v. Do you anticipate that the workload will increase, decrease, or remain constant in the upcoming 1–3 years? Is this a temporary situation?

vi. If your workload is increasing and resources will not allow for increased staffing, how do you anticipate being able to ameliorate the negative consequences of too much work and maintain a positive atmosphere?

vii. What steps can be taken to improve your program's or department's organizational efficiency within its current budget?

viii. What strategies have been used to improve the delivery of support services within the program or department?

3. Provide details on staff development and training needs. What changes in necessary skills have occurred and what is needed to meet those changes? Discuss needed in-house and/or offsite training.

D. Describe the additional data the program needs to collect annually to appropriately assess enrollment and access of this program.

    E. Describe any technology and facility needs of the program, with supporting details.

III. Success and Retention

    A. Analyze program effectiveness measures. Program effectiveness focuses on measuring a program's progress toward its goals and outcomes.

        1. State your program's goals and discuss whether you have achieved them since your last comprehensive program review. If not, why? What were the challenges? These goals should also be included in your 3-year department, division, or wing plan.

        2. Other measures of program effectiveness for service areas are satisfaction measures that are not linked to the program's student learning outcomes in Section IV of these guidelines.

    B. Please provide the following information regarding student satisfaction surveys:

        1. Briefly state how the survey was conducted (e.g., paper and pen, computer, how distributed and collected).

        2. Present each item of the survey and the response raw scores and percentages.

        3. Summarize the survey results in narrative form in one paragraph.

        4. If evaluations have been made by outside agencies, summarize their findings in no more than one-half page each.

        5. Include a copy of your satisfaction survey as an appendix.

    C. What, if any, additional data need to be collected annually to appropriately assess program effectiveness?

IV. Learning Outcomes

    A. Describe the program's student learning outcome assessment plan and process.

    B. Present findings from assessment using the 5-column assessment model (Student Services Program Student Learning Outcomes [PSLO] Assessment Model) included in this exercise.

    C. Analyze "Use of Results" conclusion (fifth column of rubric) to determine planning needs.

        1. Describe improvements/changes already made to the program, student learning outcome, and/or assessment.

        2. Describe improvements/changes that will be made to the program, student learning outcome, and/or assessment.

        3. Include timeline for any anticipated improvements/changes (e.g., 1 semester, 1 year, 3 years).

        4. Identify the resources that will be needed to make these program improvements/changes.

V. Planning

    A. Develop 3–5 strategies, based on the program's analysis of the program review areas. Strategies must include at least one 3–5-year planning strategy.

    B. Complete the planning matrix for each strategy (Three-year Planning Strategies for Years

2013–2016) included in this exercise. Address how the strategy supports the academic master plan and objectives for the Division of Student Services.

C. Identify and describe the program's staffing, facilities, and technology needs. For staffing, include hiring and staff development/training needs. For facilities and technology, the identified needs must be tied to division and campus planning documents.

Note. Adapted from Orange Coast College 2012–2013 *Student Services Comprehensive Program Review Requirements*, 2012, retrieved from http://www.orangecoastcollege.edu/student_life/deanofstu-dents/Documents/ProgramReviewRequirements20122013052412.doc. Adapted with permission.

Section IV for 2012–2013 APR and CPR
Student Services Program Student Learning Outcomes (PSLO) Assessment Model

★ *REPORTING ON 2011–2012 PSLOs* ★

Program Name: _____

Program Lead: _____ Lead Ext: _____

Program E-mail: _____ Lead E-mail: _____

Institutional Learning Outcomes: Communication; Thinking Skills; Social and Global Awareness; Personal Development and Responsibility

Program Mission Statement	Intended Student Learning Outcomes for 2011–2012	Means of Assessment & Criteria for Success	Analysis of Data Collected	Use of Results *Include any resources on Document V/Planning*
Cite the departmental or program mission statement.	What will students be able to think, know, do, or feel because of a given educational experience in a course or a program? Which ISLO is outcome linked to?	What are the specific assessment tools that established the degree and extent of what was achieved? What is the criterion (prediction) for success? For example: expected percentage of change; changes in numbers; a certain number will achieve this SLO; the number that will meet this SLO. In other words, what statement reflects how we know students learned what they were expected to learn?	Summarize findings vis-à-vis outcomes, means of assessment, and criteria for success. Include the program's process for determining who participated in the assessment and the sample size. What do the data tell us about this process in terms of goals, outcomes, and means of assessment; defined criteria for success; implementation process; and data collection?	What do the data indicate about program improvement: • What, if anything, needs to be done at the program level to improve student learning? • What resources are necessary to accomplish this? What improvements have already been made? Will the SLO remain the same for 2012–2013? Will the assessment?
	SLO #1			
	SLO #2			
	SLO #3			

Orange Coast College Program Review 2012–2013

Program: _____

Division: Student Services

Three-year Planning Strategies for Years 2013–2016 (*Section V of APR and CPR*)

Develop a minimum of three (3) strategies, at least one of which must be a 3-year strategy. The justification for each strategy below should be explicitly documented in the appropriate program review description and evaluation area (i.e., Sections II, III, and/or IV). Include strategies still in progress.

Strategies	OCC Strategic Goal(s) and Wing Goal(s) Supported	Responsible Parties	Assessment Method	Resources Needed	Source for Resources	Milestone Year 1 2013–14	Milestone Year 2 2014–15	Milestone Year 3 2015–16	Status Summary (include dates)	Specify the section of APR or CPR in which this strategy is documented
1.										
2.										
3.										

RESOURCES

Accrediting Commission for Community and Junior Colleges, Western Association of Schools and Colleges. (2011). *Rubric for evaluating institutional effectiveness – part I: Program review.* Retrieved from http://www.accjc.org/wp-content/uploads/2011/10/CoverMemoAndRevisedRubric_10-28-2011.pdf

American Public University System. (n.d.). *Glossary of assessment terms.* Retrieved August 28, 2012, from http://www.apus.edu/community-scholars/learning-outcomes-assessment/university-assessment/glossary.htm

Central Piedmont Community College. (n.d.). *Vocabulary for assessment and evaluation.* Retrieved from http://www.cpcc.edu/learningcollege/learning-outcomes/vocabulary-for-assessment-and-evaluation

Council for the Advancement of Standards in Higher Education (CAS). (n.d.). Retrieved from http://www.cas.edu

Ferance, E. (2000). *Action research.* Retrieved from http://www.lab.brown.edu/pubs/themes_ed/act_research.pdf

George Washington University. (n.d.). *Assessment glossary.* Retrieved August 28, 2012, from http://www.gwu.edu/~oapa/course_assessment/glossary.html

Higher Education Resource Hub. (n.d.). *Assessment web resources.* Retrieved August 28, 2012, from http://www.higher-ed.org/resources/Assessment.htm

Keeling, R. P. (Ed.). (2004). *Learning reconsidered: A campus-wide focus on the student experience.* Washington, DC: American College Personnel Association and National Association of Student Personnel Administrators.

Keeling, R. P. (Ed.). (2006). *Learning reconsidered 2: A practical guide to implementing a campus-wide focus on the student learning experience.* Washington, DC: American College Personnel Association, Association of College and University Housing Officers–International, Association of College Unions International, National Academic Advising Association, National Association for Campus Activities, National Association of Student Personnel Administrators, and National Intramural-Recreational Sports Association.

National Association of Student Personnel Administrators. (n.d.). *NASPA assessment and persistence conference.* Retrieved from http://www.naspa.org/programs/apc/default.cfm

North Carolina State University Planning and Analysis. (n.d.). *Internet resources for higher education outcomes assessment.* Retrieved from http://www2.acs.ncsu.edu/UPA/assmt/resource.htm

Paradise Valley College. (2008). *Assessment handbook.* Retrieved from http://www.paradisevalley.edu/sites/default/files/al_Handbook_Full_1208.pdf

REFERENCES

Accrediting Commission for Community and Junior Colleges. (2011). *Rubric for evaluating institutional effectiveness—part III: Student learning outcomes.* Retrieved from http://www.accjc. org/wp-content/uploads/2011/10/CoverMemoAndRevisedRubric_10-28-2011.pdf

Angelo, T. (1995, November). Reassessing (and defining) assessment. *AAHE Bulletin, 48*(2),7–9.

Bayless, L. A., Henning, G., Komives, S. R., & Gasser, H. S. (2012, March). *Using CAS standards for program development and assessment* [PowerPoint slides]. Retrieved from http://convention.myacpa. org/archive/programs/Louisville12/Handouts/1490/CAS%20Overview%20ACPA%202012.pdf

Bonfiglio, R. A., Nagy, L., Hillman, J., Tobin, D. M., Childress, J. T., & Johnson, R. (2009, November). *Best practices using the CAS standards: A comprehensive assessment model* [PDF document]. Retrieved from http://www.cas.edu/wp-content/uploads/2010/12/BestPractices2009.pdf

Carretta, P. (2008, June). *Using CAS standards and review process for improving student learning and program outcomes* [PowerPoint slides]. Retrieved from http://www.cas.edu/wp-content/ uploads/2010/12/NASPA_CAS_2008.ppt

Carretta, P. (2010, June). *CAS's new learning domains: Using them in your assessment work* [PowerPoint slides]. Retrieved from http://www.naspa.org/cultureofevidence/MOD7PP.pdf

Collins, K. M., & Roberts, D. M. (Eds.). (2012). *Learning is not a sprint: Assessing and documenting student leader learning in co-curricular involvement.* Washington, DC: National Association of Student Personnel Administrators.

Cosumnes River College. (n.d.). *SLO assessment portal: Background, purpose and principles of assessment.* Retrieved August 28, 2012, from http://www.crc.losrios.edu/Faculty_and_Staff/SLO_Assessment_Portal/ Instructional_SLO_Assessment_Tool-Kit/Background_Purpose_and_Principles_of_Assessment_.htm

Council for the Advancement of Standards in Higher Education (CAS). (2009a). *CAS professional standards for higher education.* Washington, DC: Author.

Council for the Advancement of Standards in Higher Education (CAS). (2009b). *CAS self-assessment guides.* Washington, DC: Author.

Council for the Advancement of Standards in Higher Education (CAS). (2012). *CAS professional standards for higher education.* Washington, DC: Author

Komives, S. R. (2006, November). *Reflections on outcomes and assessment: Applying the CAS process.* Keynote presented at the Council for the Advancement of Standards Symposium, Alexandria, VA. Retrieved from http://www.cas.edu/wp-content/uploads/2010/12/SusanKomivesCASSpeech.pdf

O'Brien, R. (2001). Um exame da abordagem metodológica da pesquisaação [An overview of the methodological approach of action research]. In R. Richardson (Ed.), *Teoria e prática da pesquisaação [Theory and practice of action research].* João Pessoa, Brazil: Universidade Federal da Paraíba.

Palmer, P.J. (1999). *Leading from within: Reflections on spirituality and leadership.* Washington, DC: Servant Leadership Press.

Riel, M. (2010). *Understanding action research.* Retrieved August 28, 2012, from http://cadres. pepperdine.edu/ccar/define.html

MODULE 8

The "Big Bang" Moment in Student Affairs: Cultures of Evidence Matter

Marguerite McGann Culp, Gwendolyn Jordan Dungy, and David P. Jones

THIS MODULE DEMONSTRATES that *Building a Culture of Evidence in Student Affairs: A Guide for Leaders and Practitioners* has implications far beyond the state of West Virginia: Moving from a culture of good intentions to a data-based culture of evidence is essential in any occupation whose members wish to be considered self-regulating professionals. In addition to inviting readers to review what they learned from the tutorial, this module gives readers an opportunity to apply their new knowledge to a case study and to identify the next steps for themselves and their departments. The module concludes with an observation that the national College Completion Agenda provides student affairs professionals with a once-in-a-generation opportunity to showcase their contributions to their institution's bottom line: student access, student success, and student completion rates.

Building a Culture of Evidence in Student Affairs was made possible through a partnership with the West Virginia Higher Education Policy Commission (WVHEPC) and the West Virginia Community and Technical College System (WVCTC) and funded by a grant from the Lumina Foundation, but it contains a universal message for student affairs professionals across the country: cultures of evidence matter. They matter to the student affairs division, to the higher education institutions that allocate resources to the division, to the students who look to student affairs for support, and to the faculty members who rely on their student affairs colleagues to design and implement programs, services, and processes that enhance the quality of each student's educational experience.

As part of the DegreeNow initiative to strengthen nonclassroom support programs and services

QUICK TIP

"Developing an understanding of student needs, program and service impacts, and opportunities for improvement makes no sense unless the results are going to be put to good use. As senior leaders, we need to be as invested in application as we are in the assessment. We need to be prepared to respond to what we learn in an appropriate and timely manner."
—*Dennis Black, vice president of student affairs, University at Buffalo (personal communication, July 16, 2012)*

for adult learners, WVHEPC and WVCTC sponsored a series of 3-day Train-the-Trainer workshops throughout 2011–2012 developed by Maggie Culp and designed for student affairs leaders. Workshop participants completed a detailed SWOT (strengths, weaknesses, opportunities, and threats) analysis of higher education in West Virginia, assessed the student affairs climate on their campuses and throughout the state, and evaluated their readiness to support DegreeNow. Participants also completed four modules designed to increase their knowledge and skill sets in four essential areas: understanding the goals of DegreeNow; designing and implementing non-classroom support services for adult learners; building and sustaining partnerships between academic and student affairs to benefit adult learners; and creating a culture of evidence in student affairs. Each module provided opportunities to apply theories and research results to real-life situations and offered dozens of examples of best practices and processes nationwide.

Train-the-Trainer graduates became the nucleus for change on individual campuses and across the state. On their home campuses, graduates designed and implemented new support programs and services for adult learners, strengthened or redirected existing programs and services, and examined current processes to determine their impact on persistence and graduation rates for adult learners. Across the state, graduates collaborated to design Leveraging DegreeNow to Support Adult Learners, an 8-hour workshop to help student affairs staff members and non-classroom support service personnel better meet the needs of adult learners. It did not take Train-the-Trainer graduates long to realize that improving their assessment skills and increasing their ability to build effective cultures of evidence in student affairs were essential steps in revitalizing the student affairs profession, strengthening support programs and services at individual institutions, and increasing the college persistence and graduation rates of adult learners.

 IN THE SPOTLIGHT

"Evidence-based defense of higher education is becoming an inescapable reality in our current environment questioning higher education's value." —*Dean Bresciani, president, North Dakota State University (personal communication, June 5, 2012)*

THE BIG BANG MOMENT

In "The New World of Student Affairs," a chapter in *Exceptional Senior Student Affairs Administrators' Leadership*, Larry Moneta and Michael L. Jackson (2011) offered four observations that readers need to keep in mind as they reflect on building a culture of evidence in student affairs: (1) the drastic reduction of student affairs operations at some institutions is a cautionary tale, not a trend; (2) if student affairs programs disappeared, students would still graduate and succeed, although in smaller numbers and with narrower perspectives; (3) student affairs professionals must remain in a continuous learning mode; and (4) the essential question is what is student affairs worth?

In West Virginia, the culture of evidence module started out as the last and smallest part of the Train-the-Trainer workshops. Participants recommended that NASPA increase the time allocated to this topic, include it in the Leveraging DegreeNow workshops, and develop a culture of evidence tutorial for professionals in nonclassroom support service areas. As one Train-the-Trainer graduate commented in his workshop evaluation, "Today's workshop was, for me, like discovering the big bang theory. And the big bang in student affairs is data! Data must be at the heart of everything we do, every story we tell. Without data, we are just well-intentioned people trying to do some good in the world, not knowledgeable professionals who can demonstrate in a concrete way that what we do makes a difference."

This tutorial is an attempt to provide student affairs professionals with an opportunity to learn how to collect, analyze, and evaluate data; how to build, nurture, and use cultures of evidence; and how to demonstrate the value of student affairs by telling its story—and telling it well. It is designed to give professionals the tools they need to demonstrate the value of the programs and services they offer, to enter and remain in a continuous learning mode, and to increase their ability to identify and respond quickly to the changing realities on their campuses.

 IN THE SPOTLIGHT

"There is no turning back. The pressure and need for accountability will continue to be a factor in all we do, and the need for assessment will grow, not go away. The clock is ticking. Colleges and universities are sometimes seen as thinkers more than doers (although by higher education standards, student affairs does a lot). But a student's life on our campuses and our opportunity to impact it is relatively short. We cannot squander the limited time we have. We need to be prepared to act as needed, and to act when needed." —*Dennis Black, vice president of student affairs, University at Buffalo (personal communication, July 6, 2012)*

BUILDING CAPACITY

Module 1 helps readers assess the infrastructure already in place to support a culture of evidence and offers guidance in developing individual and institutional baselines. In addition to putting the current emphasis on cultures of evidence in perspective, the module maps the culture of evidence journey and includes definitions, resources, and instruments to help student affairs professionals assess their readiness to become involved in assessment initiatives. The module also supplies the answer to the "WIFM" question: What's in it for me? Whether reluctant professionals are concerned about the campus credibility of student affairs or the impact building a culture of evidence will have on their own career trajectory, Module 1 clearly demonstrates that the rewards far outweigh the actual or implied risks. The final statement in the module's opening paragraph offers one of the most persuasive arguments for building capacity at all levels in student affairs and using that capacity to create cultures of evidence: "Cultures of evidence offer a degree of protection for student affairs professionals, as they document with hard data the significant contributions student affairs makes toward the institution's mission and goals."

Module 2 invites professionals to use the tools introduced in Module 1 to establish individual and team baselines, then offers practical suggestions for strengthening these baselines and filling gaps. The module provides a checklist professionals can use to assess student affairs at their institution, a PowerPoint presentation that introduces essential culture of evidence concepts, and an exercise to help student affairs professionals use Classroom Assessment Techniques (CATs) to measure the effectiveness of the programs and services they offer. Most important, the module includes powerful messages from presidents and higher education leaders about the importance of moving from a culture of good intentions to a culture of evidence in student affairs.

Module 4 is an excellent resource for readers who want to learn how to create and use developmental, learning, and program outcomes, and how to write effective rubrics. The module provides dozens of concrete examples in a variety of areas—from academic advising to orientation to women student programs—from colleges and universities across the country. The module also includes a culture of evidence table that clearly outlines the characteristics of the four major cultures in student affairs today and a robust list of resources and best practices for 24 program areas in student affairs. Finally, the module sends two important messages: (1) A culture of evidence for student affairs is broader than student learning outcomes, especially when learning is narrowly defined, and (2) student affairs professionals must document their effectiveness in mission-relevant ways, using strategies and tools that align with their institution's mission, goals, and student characteristics.

Module 5 offers a comprehensive rationale for why student affairs should consider creating a culture of evidence through ongoing assessment activities; the module does an impressive job of showing the conceptual relationship among various approaches to inquiry. The matrix that differentiates traditional research, traditional assessment, authentic assessment, and action research is masterful—a must-read for everyone in the profession. The module's explanation of credibility and utility is extremely important; its emphasis on technical know-how and "practical doing toward identified purposes that meet the needs of stakeholders" should become the golden rule for creating a culture of evidence. Too often, data collection and research become ends in themselves, and little action is taken as a result of the findings. The module also reminds readers that it is important to involve stakeholders in designing and implementing cultures of assessment. As stated in Module 5, assessment efforts at Hobart and William Smith Colleges demonstrate that "what one gives up in traditional procedural correctness, one can gain in information that is meaningful for the intended users."

A thread woven into the fabric of many modules is the importance of CAS standards in designing cultures of evidence. Module 7 picks up that thread and explores in depth the role CAS standards can play in anchoring culture of evidence initiatives. The module reinforces the importance of action research (introduced in Module 5) and reminds everyone that there is more to a culture of evidence than surveys. Module 7 advises student affairs professionals to use multiple assessment tools and cautions them that assessment is not finished simply because practitioners have completed the fifth (or sixth or seventh) step in a process. Assessment is cyclical: Student affairs professionals must continually revisit their processes to identify problems or unintended consequences, and they must use data to make decisions about processes, programs, and services.

THE LEADERSHIP EDGE

How important is leadership in culture of evidence initiatives? Module 2 stresses the importance of both leading and managing, provides concrete examples of both, and outlines strategies that senior student affairs officers (SSAOs) can use to lead and manage culture of evidence initiatives. Module 3 stresses that the team at the top plays a crucial role in preparing student affairs professionals to design and implement a culture of evidence. Leaders set the pace, help the division or department focus on what really matters, and encourage everyone to follow the data, even when the data contradict previously held (even cherished) beliefs. The module emphasizes the importance of finding and empowering champions: professionals with an interest in and the expertise to build cultures of evidence who can help to identify and coordinate assessment efforts across the division. The module also sends a clear message that a major responsibility of student affairs leaders is to make their team understand that building a culture of evidence is a continuous process and that assessment is simply a means to positively affect student success.

Module 6 illustrates the importance of leadership at all levels in a very concrete way. In one of the innovations at California State University, Sacramento, the vice president for student affairs formed the Horizontal Assessment Team, composed of midlevel staff. Team members were champions of the assessment process. Despite their hard work, however, senior administrators had to become involved to support the work and get ideas off the ground. In another innovative leadership move, the vice president tied building a culture of evidence to the Western Association of Schools and Colleges (WASC) reaccreditation process, committed the division to launching a comprehensive assessment initiative, and volunteered to have student affairs take the lead in the institutional effectiveness/ culture of evidence portion of the WASC process. As Module 6 describes, the move paid off for student affairs and for the university, and the lessons learned are invaluable for other institutions. Most importantly, the vice president excelled at assisting the student affairs team to build capacity, learn from their successes and failures, and leverage assessment data to benefit student affairs during challenging economic times.

QUICK TIP

"Understanding the diversity of assessment methods and integrating them into a broader purpose that is connected to an overall assessment plan is important. People can easily get overwhelmed and, without careful planning, can be gathering all kinds of data without really having a plan for its use. This usually results in a lot of data and limited information. People need to be thinking about what they really need to assess, have a data collection plan, and then an intentional review and appropriate use of the information. Not closing the loop and modifying practice as a result of the assessment activities is a shortcoming." —*Laura Wankel, vice president of student affairs, Northeastern University (personal communication, July 2, 2012)*

PARTNERSHIPS

A central theme of *Building a Culture of Evidence in Student Affairs: A Guide for Leaders and Practitioners* is the essential role that developing and maintaining partnerships plays in creating cultures of evidence. Module 2 talks about the importance of internal and external partnerships to train staff and share data. Module 3 encourages SSAOs to support partnerships, build relationships, and collaborate with others across campus to develop and sustain a culture of evidence. Module 5 offers an example of how everyone benefits when a university and a community college collaborate on a research project to better understand community college students. Module 6 describes the important partnerships within student affairs and between student affairs and the Office of Institutional Research that anchored the culture of evidence initiative at California State University, Sacramento.

Module 7 reminds student affairs professionals that faculty partnerships are the building blocks of an effective culture of evidence initiative. Partnerships matter. They supplement the skill sets that already exist in student affairs. They help student affairs professionals view what they do and how they do it through a different lens. They develop student affairs champions outside the division, champions with a vested interest in seeing student affairs succeed. They educate the college community about student affairs and its contributions to the institution. Most important, partnerships send a clear message that collaboration and transparency, not competition and isolation, are the keys to institutional success.

> ### QUICK TIP
>
> "Student affairs professionals need to collect data on what we don't know rather than to only collect data to validate and reaffirm what we think we know. We tend to get feedback from those attending a program, but those in populations targeted for attendance who did not attend should be periodically surveyed as well." —*Ken Stoner, assistant vice chancellor for student affairs, The University of Tennessee, Knoxville (personal communication, June 17, 2012)*

CONCLUSION

The national College Completion Agenda gives student affairs an opportunity to shine a spotlight on the significant role that nonclassroom support services, programs, and processes play in helping

> ### QUICK TIP
>
> "To get faculty interested requires first showing and demonstrating interest in *their* concerns. For example, at Texas A&M, student affairs began an extensive longitudinal study about what out-of-class activities most complement rather than compete with academic success. In addition to fascinating results, faculty developed a new interest in the study of this topic, which opened countless doors and started us down a very different path of discovery and inquiry—together."
> —*Dean Bresciani, president, North Dakota State University (personal communication, June 5, 2012)*

QUICK TIP

"Too often, a student affairs assessment program is run by one person on staff and it becomes their mission. Others respect what they are doing, but don't learn the "how" or "why" of the process. We need to expand appreciation for assessment processes to a broader campus audience and make sure that there is an ongoing system in place that will not just survive, but can thrive if the key staff person leaves the campus or moves on to another role." —*Dennis Black, vice president of student affairs, University at Buffalo (personal communication, July 6, 2012)*

higher education institutions increase persistence and completion rates for all students. To take full advantage of this opportunity, student affairs divisions across the country must demonstrate their value to students, to faculty, and to their institution by providing a data-based answer to the age-old questions: What is student affairs worth, and why should we allocate resources to it? Creating strong cultures of evidence that ask and answer challenging questions about student affairs programs and services, cultures that include vertical as well as horizontal assessment, is an important step toward focusing attention on the many contributions student affairs makes to the College Completion Agenda and to higher education institutions throughout the country.

APPLY THE CONCEPTS

Exercise 8.1—*Applying What You Have Learned: A Case Study*

Modules 1–7 provide an introduction to designing and implementing a culture of evidence in student affairs. The modules offer insights and lessons learned from seasoned higher education professionals across the country, including many who were pioneers in early assessment and culture of evidence initiatives. Now it is your turn to assess and apply what you have learned. Take a few minutes to reflect on the lessons in each of the modules, and then complete the following case study. Use your performance on the case study to identify the modules you need to revisit, and determine the next steps you need to take to strengthen your ability to design and implement a culture of evidence in your area.

Charles River University (CRU), located an hour south of the state's primary metropolitan center, was recently recognized by the major newspaper for the superb internship opportunities it offers to its students, opportunities that benefit the students as well as the businesses and industries at which they intern. The day after the article appeared, the senior student affairs officer (SSAO) received an email from CRU's president, congratulating the division on the positive press for the program and the university. The president asked the SSAO what data student affairs had to help the university evaluate the effect of this program on student learning and eventual career placement. The SSAO tells the president that the student affairs division is in the preliminary stages of building a structure to assess the impact of all of its programs, and he looks forward to sharing progress reports with her throughout the year. The SSAO has invited you to be a part of the Student Affairs Culture of Evidence Task Force. In the following case study exercises, show how you would use the knowledge you gained from reading *Building a Culture of Evidence in Student Affairs: A Guide for Leaders and Practitioners* in your work with the task force.

In Module 1, you learned that mature cultures of evidence share four essential characteristics. You hope to persuade the task force that student affairs needs to create a model that reflects the best elements of cultures of evidence already in place at higher education institutions across the country. To prepare for the first task force meeting, take a few minutes to list the four essential characteristics of a mature culture of evidence. Write a sentence or two to explain to your colleagues on the task force the importance of each characteristic to student affairs at your institution.

Characteristics of a Mature Culture of Evidence	Significance/Importance of This Characteristic
Characteristic #1	
Characteristic #2	
Characteristic #3	
Characteristic #4	

Module 2 focuses on how to address the challenges institutions and individuals face in establishing a culture of evidence baseline. List five strategies, in priority order, that you believe the SSAO should use at CRU to strengthen the student affairs division and the professionals who work there before initiating the culture of evidence design and implementation processes.

1.
2.
3.
4.
5.

Module 3 highlights the importance of the student affairs leadership team and discusses how to prepare the team to lead culture of evidence initiatives. As a task force member, what five recommendations would you offer to the SSAO to help her prepare the team at the top (e.g., associate and assistant vice presidents, deans) and the team in the middle (e.g., directors, coordinators, and program heads) to lead a culture of evidence initiative?

	Recommendation	Rationale
1		
2		
3		
4		
5		

Three members of the task force arrive for the first meeting with examples of what their areas are doing to create cultures of evidence. The director of counseling offers a copy of the annual report for the counseling area; the director of services for students with disabilities contributes an example of a rubric that the department recently developed; and the director of admissions provides an example of a student learning outcome for his area. Review these materials, which are provided at the end of this exercise. Take a few minutes to think about what you learned in Module 4, and then offer advice to the task force about the three items.

	Strengths	Suggestions for Improvement	Usefulness to the Task Force
Annual report			
Rubric			
Student learning outcome			

At the first task force meeting, your colleagues ask you to develop a presentation for the next meeting that brings members up to speed on the major approaches to assessment and research. After reviewing Module 5, you design a table that focuses on traditional and authentic assessment, traditional research, and action research. Take a few minutes to think about Module 5, and then complete the table below.

	Definition	Tools/Methods
Traditional assessment		
Authentic assessment		
Traditional research		
Action research		

Module 6 chronicled the six-year evolution of a culture of evidence at a major state university. Think about the lessons shared in the module; identify the five lessons to which the task force should pay special attention, and describe how CRU can use these lessons in designing and implementing a culture of evidence that meets the needs of its own student affairs division.

	Lessons Learned	How CRU Can Apply These Lessons
1		
2		
3		
4		
5		

Experience has taught you that the need for assessment typically arises from pressure to evaluate a specific program or answer a specific question. In the case of CRU, the president wants to understand the effect of the internship program on student learning. From reading Module 7, however, you realize that an effective assessment process is a cyclical one designed to strengthen programs, services, and processes. You also believe that action research is an approach to information gathering and decision making that might work at CRU—if you can educate your colleagues about its use and importance. Before introducing the topic at a task force meeting, take a few minutes to organize your thoughts on how to use action research to generate answers to the original question asked by the president: What data currently exist to help the university evaluate the impact of internships on students' learning and eventual career placement?

1. Problem to address, area to examine, and/or essential question.
2. Data to collect and collection strategies.
3. Strategies for analyzing, evaluating, and interpreting the data.
4. Strategies for developing an action plan that outlines what you plan to do in response to the data.
5. Strategies to evaluate the impact of the action research and the action(s) taken as a result of the research.

How Did You Do?

The process you just completed offers a snapshot of what you learned from *Building a Culture of Evidence in Student Affairs: A Guide for Leaders and Practitioners.* To assess your performance, review each of your responses, and then use the following chart to score your efforts.

	Emerging	**Developing**	**Proficient**	**Exemplary**
Module 1 Mature characteristics of cultures of evidence	Able to list one characteristic	Able to list two characteristics	Able to list all four characteristics, but referred to Module 1 two or more times	Able to list all four characteristics without referring back to Module 1 more than once
Module 2 Core elements of cultures of evidence	Able to list one or two strategies	Able to list three strategies	Able to list four or five strategies, but referred to Module 2 two or more times	Able to identify five strategies without referring back to Module 2 more than once
Module 3 Action plans	Able to identify one recommendation and the rationale to support it	Able to identify two recommendations and the rationales to support them	Able to identify four or five recommendations and the rationales to support them, but referred to Module 3 two or more times	Able to identify five recommendations and the rationales to support them without referring back to Module 3 more than once
Module 4 Managing a culture of evidence	Able to recognize that counting heads and measuring student satisfaction (see Annual Report for the Counseling Department, Charles River University) are only small pieces of the culture of evidence puzzle	Able to understand the limits of the counting heads approach and the underlying strength of the descriptive rubric (see Rubric to Assess the Ability of Students with Disabilities Who Completed a Series of Workshops Sponsored by Student Affairs to Locate, Evaluate, and Apply Information)	Able to recognize the limits of the counting heads and satisfaction survey approaches, the power of a descriptive rubric, and the strengths and weaknesses of the student learning outcome (see Student Learning Outcome for the Admissions Office, Charles River University)	(1) Able to achieve a "Proficient" rating and (2) confident that you can develop one learning outcome and identify one assessment strategy for your area that includes a rubric
Module 5 Research approaches	Able to define one or two terms but struggle to describe two or more major tools or methods associated with the terms	Able to define two research terms and easily describe two or more major tools or methods associated with the terms	Able to define all four terms but find it difficult to describe two or more major tools or methods associated with each term	Able to define all four terms and provide examples of at least two tools or methods associated with each term
Module 6 Lessons learned from the California State University, Sacramento, case study	Able to formulate two lessons from the case study and describe how to apply these lessons	Able to formulate three lessons from the case study and describe how to apply these lessons	Able to formulate four lessons from the case study and describe how to apply these lessons	Able to formulate five lessons from the case study and describe how to apply these lessons
Module 7 Action research cycle	Unable to identify or apply any action research step	Able to identify and apply one or two action research steps	Able to identify and apply three or four action research steps	Able to identify and apply five action research steps

Annual Report for the Counseling Department, Charles River University

The counseling department provided services to 2,322 students (unduplicated head count).

- ○ 34% of the students participated in career counseling activities.
- ○ 31% requested assistance with educational planning.
- ○ 25% were referred or referred themselves for personal counseling.
- ○ 10% participated in support groups for students on academic probation.
- ○ In the annual survey of student satisfaction, students who used counseling services rated their satisfaction levels as follows:
  - ✳ Very satisfied: 11%
  - ✳ Somewhat satisfied: 24%
  - ✳ Neither satisfied nor dissatisfied: 41%
  - ✳ Somewhat dissatisfied: 13%
  - ✳ Very dissatisfied: 7%
  - ✳ No response: 4%

Rubric to Assess the Ability of Students with Disabilities Who Completed a Series of Workshops Sponsored by Student Affairs to Locate, Evaluate, and Apply Information

	Emerging	Developing	Proficient	Exemplary
Use Degree Audit (a program to track progress toward a degree)	Can access audit but not understand the information it contains	Able to access degree audit and understand about 50% of the information it contains	Can access audit, understand 90% of the information it contains, and use the information with assistance to construct a basic individual education plan (IEP)	Can access the audit, understand and apply all the information it contains, and build a sophisticated IEP
Use FACTS.org (a program to help students select a major, learn about state colleges and universities, understand the transfer process, etc.)	Can locate but not able to navigate	Able to find and navigate FACTS.org with some assistance	Can locate and navigate FACTS.org and use the information with assistance to construct a basic IEP	Can locate and navigate FACTS.org and use the information to build a sophisticated IEP
Develop an individual education plan (IEP) that incorporates Degree Audit and FACTS.org information	Understands what an IEP is but cannot develop one	Develops a basic IEP that reflects a minimal grasp of Degree Audit or FACTS.org data	Able to develop an IEP with assistance that demonstrates the ability to incorporate Degree Audit and FACTS.org data	Able to develop an IEP without assistance that demonstrates a sophisticated ability to apply Degree Audit and FACTS.org data

Student Learning Outcome for the Admissions Office, Charles River University

Note. This outcome supports Charles River University's General Learning Outcome #4: Students will formulate strategies to locate, evaluate, and apply information.

Learning Outcome	Assessment Strategy
Students who use online admissions will demonstrate that they have learned how to navigate the Admissions and Registration website and to locate and evaluate information. Students will demonstrate that they are able to follow directions, correctly complete the admissions process, schedule an orientation session, and check their residency status.	Point of service: Build evaluation components into the A&R website that allows users to evaluate the site's effectiveness and what they learned while using it. Annual: Conduct focus groups during which students respond to open-ended questions to determine: • The A&R functions for which they used the web • What they learned as a result of using the A&R website • How A&R could make its website a more effective teaching tool

REFERENCE

Moneta, L., & Jackson, M. L. (2011). The new world of student affairs. In G. J. Dungy & S. E. Ellis (Eds.), *Exceptional senior student affairs administrators' leadership: Strategies and competencies for success* (pp. 1–14). Washington, DC: National Association of Student Personnel Administrators.

INDEX